The Black Christian Experience

THE
BLACK
CHRISTIAN
EXPERIENCE

Emmanuel L. McCall, Compiler

BROADMAN PRESS
Nashville, Tennessee

Library of Congress Catalog Card Number: 72-79173
Dewey Decimal Classification: 260
Printed in the United States of America.

Foreword

Believing that the black church tradition has something positive to offer American Christianity, the Department of Work with National Baptists of the Home Mission Board, Southern Baptist Convention, sponsored a conference entitled "Sharing the Uniqueness of the Black Church Experience." This conference was held at the Home Missions Week emphases at the Glorieta and Ridgecrest Baptist Assemblies in the summer of 1971. We had two purposes in mind.

First, we wished to provide information to Southern Baptists concerning the black church. Secondly, we wanted to help black Baptists understand and appreciate their heritage, hoping that by doing so they could accentuate the positive and eliminate the negative.

Seven topics were selected. Fourteen men recognized as having some expertise in the selected areas of discipline were chosen. Seven men delivered addresses on these topics at each assembly.

Because of the positive, informative benefits we have selected six of these presentations for this volume. To these six we have added two lecturers by Reverend Otis Moss, delivered at the annual session of the Baptist Unified Christian Leadership Conference in Kentucky, and a final chapter written by the compiler.

We express the hope that through the printed page American Christendom may appreciatively understand the black religious heritage and maximize its use to the glory of God.

EMMANUEL L. McCALL

Contents

1·Black Church Distinctives

OTIS MOSS, JR.

For better or for worse in the North American section of the Western hemisphere, we do have what can be relatively designated as the black church and the white church. The black church is the product of one of the agonies in Christian history. There are four compelling agonies in Christendom. These are: war, anti-Semitism, capitalism, and racism.

All of these are serious challenges to the Christian faith. The issue of race, however, has caused the American church to lose much respect in the modern world. It is at this point that the black church might be referred to as the remnant church, the last creative force, maybe; and maybe the last best hope for a redeeming faith in our time. But I use the word *maybe* because no theology has the last word. God has the last word. Therefore, no matter what I might think, no matter what C. Eric Lincoln or James Cone or any of the others of this age giving interpretations to the popular theme of blackness might think, one of the things we must keep in mind is that we do not have the last word. We never know when and where God might appear and do the impossible. Therefore, it is dangerous for any of us to say conclusively, "This is it." God is still the Alpha and Omega of history.

Let me hurry on to say a few other things. The concept of "soul" and "soul music" had its roots in the black church. Whether it is Mahalia Jackson or Aretha Franklin; whether it is Roland Hayes or Stevie Wonder; whether it is William Warfield or the Jackson Five, soul music has its roots in the black church.

Those popular vocalists and musicians today who are gathering a fortune are really indebted to the black church. I don't know if

9

they have paid their dues lately or not, but they got it "at home" and "down home." When I listen to James Brown, I am reminded of the singing of Deacon Will Truett at the Old Mt. Olive Baptist Church in Troupe County, Georgia. The mailing address was La Grange but that was a long way from Old Mt. Olive.

It is true to history then to say that the agonies of racism are the birth pangs of the black church. The black church is an indictment and a commitment in Western culture.

This thing we call the black church (and this is a limited definition) is really "that Christian fellowship whose origin or establishment, administration, function, life, order and structure are exclusively in the hands of black people." In a sense we are talking about a relative and limited fellowship. These congregations or fellowships are primarily black Baptists founded as early as 1776 and a few years before: the A.M.E.'s (African Methodists Episcopals), and the A.M.E. Zion. The C.M.E. (Colored Methodist Episcopal) was organized by white folk to keep black folk out of the white church. That's why they were called Colored Methodists in the beginning, but in 1957 they changed their name to Christian Methodist. So they were Colored Methodists historically and Christian Methodists by legislation.

In addition to the classical denominations among black people there are also the sects, the cults, the holiness, and other church bodies which have been numerous in the urban culture. In 1807 an African Presbyterian Church was founded. In 1818 the Black Episcopal Church was organized. In 1829 a black Congregational Church was founded. But the Baptists and the Methodists had the greatest appeal to the masses of black people in North America, and there are reasons for this.

In the highly sophisticated, liturgical church everything was organized two and three hundred years before they got to that moment. The order of worship—the prayers and everything else—was all organized two or three hundred years before the hour of worship or the experience of worship. The prayers were all written out in the book. The slaves could not carry a prayer book around in their hip pocket out in the cotton fields, in order to say: "Lord bless the Queen of England and all of her cabinet. Bless the government and Parliament." They didn't have the time to go through all of that. In fact, they were not able to read.

But as the sun made its journey, or as the earth made its revolution, they looked toward the setting of the sun and said:

> This evening our heavenly Father, it's once more and again that this your humble servant, knee bent and body bowed, one more time. And as I bow, I want to thank you for my last night's lying down. I want to thank you for a guardian angel that you sent to watch over me all night long while I slumbered and slept. I want to thank you because you touched me with a finger of love this morning, and woke me up on due time. I yet have the activity of my limbs and my tongue was not cleaved to the roof of my mouth. I was yet left in a gospel land and a Bible reading country. . . ."

Then they looked around at a mean boss man and said: ". . . Where mens and womens won't do right."

The black church was founded in slavery, through a certain kind of freedom that was invisibly communicated from God to man which the slave master could not catch. While we were, in terms of geography, a distant and long way removed from "Jerusalem," God planted in our souls the seeds of a "new Jerusalem."

The early establishment of the classical black church was by slaves, ex-slaves, and some free black people during the era of slavery. This is why some of these churches are called *African* Methodist Episcopal, *African* Methodist Episcopal Zion, First *African* Baptist. Of course, some cultural changes took place. I will not take the time to delve into this, but it would be interesting for someone to get some background on the stages we went through. There was the African stage, the colored stage, the Negro stage, and now back to the black stage.

When our memories were yet closed to the coasts of West Africa, we yet had not only an African culture but even in our conversation, in our own tradition, we had a living memory of Africa. But then the islands of the sea were infused in the slavery experience causing some people to say, "We are from the islands, we are not Africans," and they were right. So there was a decision that maybe "colored" was more inclusive, for that would include Africa and the islands of the seas. Somebody else said "We are neither *African* or *colored*. We are *Negro.*" Today we say we are just *black.*

Are Black and White Churches Different?

The distinct difference between the black church and the white church must be remembered. Even though we get some literature from them once in a while, there is a difference.

What are some of these differences? In the first place the black church is the church of the oppressed and the white church is the church of the oppressor. Now this isn't to say that everybody identified with the white church is by the fact of identification an oppressor, but it is the institution of the oppressor. There is a difference. You see, the songs of the Hebrews in Babylon will always be different from those of the Babylonians of Babylon. The songs of the people *in the world* and yet not *of the world* will always be different from the songs of the people of the world. The Babylonian could sing one kind of song, but the Hebrews said:

> By the rivers of Babylon, there we sat down, yea, we wept, when we remembered Zion. We hanged our harps upon the willows in the midst thereof. For there they that carried us away captive required of us a song; and they that wasted us required of us mirth, saying, Sing us one of the songs of Zion. How shall we sing the Lord's song in a strange land? If I forget thee, O Jerusalem, let my right hand forget her cunning. If I do not remember thee, let my tongue cleave to the roof of my mouth; if I prefer not Jerusalem above my chief joy"
> (Ps. 137:1-6).

But even though they said they could not sing the songs of Zion in a strange land, *they ended up creating a song.* The song was different in harmony and in melody from the songs of the Babylonians. So we have a song different from the Indians, different from the white man, and different from the Africans back home. It was a unique song. It was the song of the oppressed. "I'm So Glad That Trouble

Don't Last Always" wasn't an Indian song, nor a European song, nor was it an African song; it was God's song in our hearts in a strange land under the yoke of oppression.

There is a second difference. The practicing religion of the black church is a theology of survival, generally. It is also a carrier of the black folk culture. The practicing religion of the white church, with certain exceptions, has been American culture and racism. Ours is a theology of hope. I must underscore the fact that the black church is the carrier of black folk culture. Some people have almost forgotten that today. If you want true authentic American black culture, you must go to the black church. With no offense intended, you can't find this in the Catholic Church, or the Episcopal Church. How can a Mahalia Jackson be born in a Catholic Church? She would have to teach them that kind of music. How can a Martin Luther King, Jr., be nurtured in the Church of England? It would be a contradiction of the church itself. The church would blow up in confusion. Can you imagine someone coming to St. Paul's Cathedral and whooping like C. L. Franklin or a whole lot of us other Baptists?

The black church has been distinguished greatly by a dynamic and free pulpit. The white church has had a static circumscribed pulpit. The white pastor preaches, wondering if the trustees and deacons will approve. The black preacher is primarily concerned with whether God will approve.

Let me point out something else. When we didn't have any lawyers to interpret the meaning of constitutional rights, property rights, and human rights, the black pulpit was our defense. Even though the black preacher was not knowledgeable in the Justinian Code or the Code of Hammurabi, or the dynamics of Roman and Greek culture, even though he had not been to a law school, he did know "you've got to reap what you sow." When we didn't have any lawyers, the pulpit was our defense.

When we didn't have any professors, any Ph.D.'s, the pulpit became a station of education. It couldn't do this without dynamics and freedom. It is no wonder that you could go to sleep easily in

First Baptist downtown, but you couldn't go to sleep too easily at Shady Grove. Even when you were not *with* the program, something would happen in the "amen corner," in the choir, and in the pulpit that would keep you awake. Sometimes it was not only impossible to go to sleep, it was not even safe to go to sleep.

The black church is greatly distinguished then by a dynamic and free pulpit, and we should use every ounce of energy necessary to maintain that freedom and dynamic.

The great divisions of the white church in America have been divisions created over the race question. The great divisions in the black church have been over leadership struggles. We haven't had any great theological controversies in the black church. You may not agree with this, but you can believe almost anything and say it sweetly and just about get away with it. When have you heard of a conference of black Baptists convening over a theological issue? We have done a lot of things on psychology and sociology, and theology incidentally got involved. Therefore, the controversies of the black church, although they have had their theological implications and indications, did not arise from our raising great theological issues. Quite often they were great and disturbing sociological issues.

What Has the Black Church Done for Black People?

First, the black church has been a vehicle of creative hope. Second, it has provided integrity. Integrity means wholeness. When the world and the society in which we lived was constantly tearing us apart, the church continued to help us to get it together, to "get it all together." When we were torn apart all the week, for a few fleeting moments in that worship service we had an experience of togetherness. How were we torn apart? Somebody called us "boy" and we were over fifty, having lived a half century. Somebody called us "nigger" and that tore us apart. Somebody called us "darky" and that tore us apart. Somebody called us "granny" and we knew they were not our grandchildren. Somebody would call us "crazy." Someone would call us "mean, evil, and low down." Sometimes the children simply said "him" and the wife said "that one." But for a few fleeting moments in the "household of integrity," the black church, we got the notion that "I've Got a New Name Over in Zion." The black church has provided integrity.

The black church also provided social unity. It has provided a social house, a culture center, a freedom house. It has provided limited educational support. It has provided a meaningful spiritual legacy. The thrust for freedom by black Americans has found a home in the black church. Please remember that our mass meetings were not held in a cathedral or a synagogue. You remind some people of that. The operational base for Dr. Martin Luther King, Jr., was the black church.

Dr. Howard Thurman in his *The Luminous Darkness* speaks eloquently concerning the black church and how it provides integrity and a sense of "somebodiness" to black people. He has this to say.

> It is a great irony that the Negro church has figured so largely as a rallying center for the civil rights movement in the South primarily because of its strategic position as an institution in Negro life; it has not become a civil rights rallying center because of its religious ethical teaching as such. But the logic of the impact of the religious experience in the Negro church made it inevitable that it would become such a center. For a long time the Negro church was the one place in the life of a people which was comparatively free from interference by the white community. A man may be buffeted about by his environment, or may be regarded as a nobody in the general community; a woman may be a nurse in a white family in which the three-year-old child in her care calls her by her first name, thus showing quite unconsciously the contempt in which she is held by his parents. When this Negro man and this Negro woman come to their church, however, for one terribly fulfilling moment they are somebody.[1]

The black church has converted oppression into poetry, exploitation into creative force, humiliation into a hunger for justice, haunting fears into hymns of faith. If this church is to remain relevant, it must convert a praying people into a positive power-conscious people. Prayer must find fulfilment in revolutionary action. Remember that prayer without action is empty. Remember also that action without prayer is dangerous.

The black church, then, was born in a political storm or a social storm, and I think it can do its best witnessing when the storm is raging.

Have you ever thought about the fact that without a psychiatrist, we withstood things that send most people to insane asylums. We didn't have the benefits of psychiatric counseling at the point of death, but the black preacher at the funeral service became the psychiatrist, without fee. The black church kept the black race from committing suicide. When we were living under the conditions of genocide (and we still are), the black church kept us alive on the inside and we outlived, in many instances, the slave master; took care of him and his children. At the same time, we survived with less than half enough. We didn't need any dope. We didn't need any "speed." We didn't need any marijuana. You see, dope is the medicine of a slave. With all of the people talking about "revolution" (and I believe in it) you tell them that as long as they are on dope you will never have a revolution. Dope is designed to keep you enslaved. We have to say to the black community, "We need somebody to transport hope, because we already have too many importing dope." The black church ought to be, should be the vehicle of hope in a hopeless world.

Some black people have gotten confused on this and they are trying to make our churches European in style and content. Even many of our seminaries are sending out seminarians and seminary graduates trying to preach like other folk. "Stand right there and don't move." "Turn the page." "Quote a little verse and sit down." "When you can do that, we might invite you to give some remarks in our meetings sometimes."

Let me give you two examples of what I'm trying to suggest. Suppose Fred Shuttlesworth in Birmingham, Ralph Abernathy in Birmingham, and Martin Luther King, Jr., in Birmingham facing Bull Conner had pulled out a prayer book, reading in Latin, and then called upon a European-styled choir director to lead the group in singing "A Mighty Fortress Is Our God." All of the water hoses of Bull Conner would have washed the whole freedom movement down the very streets of history. The angels would have cried, and the devils would have giggled with glee.

Suppose somebody who has all of the fundamentals from the book in music, was singing "Sometimes I Feel Like a Motherless Child." Let's say that the person has a degree in music, and that's wonderful. Let's say that they know all about A sharp and A flat, when to make a crescendo and when to make a diminuendo (whatever that is), but one thing is lacking, they just can't sing. Some folks are trying to make us believe that our singing is uncultured; and because they can't sing, they elevate their nonsinging to the level of sophisticated culture and got us putting down our good singing for their no-singing. Such a person would sing "Sometimes I Feel Like a Motherless Child" only with culture but no feeling.

On the other hand, take somebody else who knows what it means to walk to school with a lunch wrapped up in a little brown greasy bag; somebody who knows what it means to be required to move but nowhere to move; somebody who knows what it means to be required to pay-up but with nothing to pay down; somebody who knows what it means "to wet their pillows with the midnight dew," without any instruments but the music in their own souls. They can stand in the scorching heat of the noonday sun, bow their heads, and in the experience of their commitment cry out: "Sometimes I feel like a motherless child, a long ways from home."

Revolution starts in the heart after revelation. When the houses are burning down, revolution says we are "looking for a city that has foundations whose builder and maker is God." This ought to be the message of the black church in a confused world.

2•Black Church History

LEON L. TROY AND EMMANUEL L. McCALL

When the first slaves arrived in America in 1619, the idea prevailed that one Christian should not hold another Christian in bondage. This was an unwritten law. Among the theological debates of the 1600's and 1700's was the question of whether or not the slave had a soul. This issue was resolved by deciding that the slaves had a soul but it was of a lower nature. "As one member of a much older slave society put it, some men were 'slaves by nature.' " [1] There was a long hesitancy among American churchmen to even attempt the evangelization of slaves and Indians. To do so was to acknowledge "the assumption of the inner sameness of all men." [2]

"Many slaveholders felt that no matter how much conversion might benefit the Negroes' souls, it could only make them worse slaves." [3] They would thereafter press for freedom, status, and equality. History has proven that the most avid champions of human dignity have been converted slaves and Christian blacks.

Some whites disavowed the conversion of slaves because of the fear of equality in heaven. "The Reverend Francis Le Jau reported from South Carolina that a lady had inquired of him, 'Is it possible that any of my slaves could go to Heaven and must I meet them there?' " [4]

Another excuse that was used to avoid the Christianizing of slaves was that they were void of capacity to learn. Reverend Samuel Davies in a lecture to Virginia slave owners corrected this misnomer when he said, "Your Negroes may be ignorant and stupid as to divine Things, not for Want of Capacity, but for Want of Instruction; not through their Perverseness, but through your Negligence." [5] Cotton Mather echoed a similar theme in his *Small Offers*

Towards the Tabernacle in the Wilderness by saying, "They (the slave are kept only as Horses or Oxen to do our Drudgeries, but their Souls, which are as white and good as those of other Nations, their Souls are not look'd after, but are Destroyed for lack of Knowledge. This is a desparate Wickedness." [6]

This controversy lasted until 1667, when the Virginia legislature passed a law declaring, "that baptism did not alter the condition of a person as to his bondage or freedom." [7] This act helped to remove the Christian religion as a legal barrier to slavery in the colonies.

The first Roman Catholic priest and missionaries in Maryland believed it to be their duty to enlighten slaves in the line of church doctrine and other religious instructions. However, this policy was not generally true of Roman Catholic pioneers in this area.

The Protestant church had even a greater lag than that of the Roman Catholic in this area. The English seemed to be interested in finding new homes in America. They thought of the blacks, not as the object of Christian love, but rather as a tool with which they might reach their end. It was a general feeling among the English that the closer to *servitude* that the slave was kept, the more useful he would be as a laborer; therefore, little concern was given for his spiritual needs.

England, desiring to maintain its hold on the colonies in America and to win more holdings in America from other nations, especially Spain and France, organized the Society for Promoting Christian Knowledge (SPCK) in 1699 and the Society for the Propagation of the Gospel in Foreign Parts (SPG) in 1701. The SPG gave much attention to the Christianizing of Indians and Negroes, both the Negroes who were free and those who were slaves. "The history of the SPG and its ally, the bishop of London, at times seems to consist largely of a series of hortatory sermons, instructions, pamphlets, reports, and letters of admonition." [8]

The geographical and communicative distance between England and America was another of these "mysterious ways in which God moved," for the religious leadership in England could not accept

American attitudes towards slavery and used its influence for the good of the slaves. Winthrop Jordan suggests how difficult the communication was in his account of a Christian black named David.

David was given permission by the Countess of Huntingdon, a Londoner who owned slaves in Georgia, to preach. James Habersham a Savannah merchant secretly slipped David out to England and sent this explanation of the near lynching David almost received:

> "His Business was to preach a Spiritual Deliverance to these People, not a temporal one, but he is, if I am not mistaken, very proud, and very superficial, and conceited, and I must say it's a pity, that any of these People should ever put their feet in England, where they get totally spoiled and ruined [David had been to England] both in Body and Soul, through a mistaken kind of compassion because they are black, while many of our own colour and Fellow Subjects, are starving through want and Neglect. We know these People better than you do." [9]

Effects of the Great Awakening

The SPG was not to be credited with being the champion of slave freedom either by their influence upon the masters or the slaves. They did stir religious concern that paved the way for the religious experiences that came in the Great Awakening. The Great Awakening was the American version of the spiritual rebirth occurring in England in the early 1700's. This was prompted, not by a rebirth in theology, but by a rebirth and reformation of liturgy. A Congregationalist, Isaac Watts (known to most blacks as "Old Dr. Watts") developed a modern hymnody which allowed congregational participation. The more original versions, metered hymns, are still used in many black congregations but with the black charisma added.

The preaching of the Wesley brothers, John and Charles, and men of their flavor was also part of the reformation of the liturgy. Worship came down from its high-church plateau and became the heart throb of the common people. The worship of the middle and lower classes was greatly enhanced. The Wesleys imported their brand of religious expression to America and had an even more successful result. They, along with such men as William Tennent, Sr., Gilbert Tennent, George Whitefield, Jonathan Edwards, and Samuel Davies, caused much spiritual stirring.

Their meetings were characterized by long, emotional sermons, shouting, fainting, leaping, laughing, jerking, rolling, barking, and many religious expressions previously unheard of and in some quarters unappreciated. The extremes between those desiring quiet formal worship and those caught up in the revival spirit led to divisions within denominations; the "Old Side" excluded the "New Side" among Presbyterians, the "Old Lights" excluded the "New Lights" among Congregationalists.

Expecially in the frontier regions and South did this new religious expression gain strength. The camp meetings, brush-arbor meetings, and tent meetings were not only the scenes for religious expressions, but also the *sitz en leben* (situation in life) for the creativity of new religious expressions. For example, "spirituals" both white and Negro had their birth out of the hardships and loneliness of both the frontier and slave situations. While there is a marked difference between these two types of spirituals, their rootage is similar.

Perhaps the most unnoticed result of the Great Awakening was the fact that the debate over whether or not the Negro had a soul ceased. Slaves were included in the camp meetings, brush-arbor meetings, and general evangelistic endeavors. Mass conversions among the slave population was evidenced. This prompted the need of continuing worship opportunities. Several developments can be noted:

1. On plantations where the owners were opposed to the Christianizing of the Negro, religious exercise was prohibited. This led to secret meetings held in woods or other places of safety. Some features begun or developed out of those experiences continue even now establishing tempo by the use of tub bottoms or hollow logs as drums, the singing of metered hymns, the charismatic rise of slave preachers to guide the worship and do the preaching.

2. On plantations where the masters were Christian or sympa-

thetic to the Christianizing of slaves several options developed. Some plantations had churches for the slaves. They were often presided over by a local white preacher. On occasions a slave preacher would be allowed to "exercise his gift." He would be supervised by a white person to avoid the risk of having the preacher gain preeminence or preach insurrection. The slave preacher's role was often no more than that of an "exhorter." Often he only complimented the main sermon either by warming up the congregation or providing afterthoughts.

The reasons for some slave owners permitted the Christianizing of their slaves was mixed. Some were genuinely concerned about the total development of their slaves. Others, however, were moved by economic exploitability. Some missionaries advanced the notion that Christianizing the Negro would make him a better slave rather than a worse one. He would be more docile, "tamed," less subject to rebellion than formerly so. One to advance such an idea was Dean George Berkeley who in 1725 tried "to convince American planters 'that it would be of Advantage to their Affairs, to have Slaves who should obey in all Things their Masters according to the Flesh, not with Eye-service as Men-pleasers, but in Singleness of Heart as fearing God: That Gospel Liberty consists with temporal Servitude; and that their Slaves would only become better Slaves by being Christians.' " [10]

A further statement was issued by the bishop of London in 1727. In a letter "To the Masters and Mistresses of Families in the English Plantations Abroad," he said:

> Christianity, and the embracing of the Gospel, does not make the least Alteration in Civil Property, or in any of the Duties which belong to Civil Relations; but in all these Respects, it continues Persons just in the same State as it found them. The Freedom which Christianity gives, is a Freedom from the Bondage of Sin and Satan, and from the Dominion of Men's Lusts and Passions and inordinate Desires; but as to their *outward* Condition, whatever that was before, whether bound or free, their being baptiz'd, and becoming Christians, makes no manner of Change in it. . . . And so far is Christianity from

discharging Men from the Duties of the Station and Condition in which it found them, that it lays them under stronger Obligations to perform those Duties with the greatest Diligence and Fidelity.[11]

Those slave owners who approved the Christianizing of their slaves out of economic expediency required a high morality content as well as an other-worldly emphasis. The slave was enjoined not to be wrathful or licentious; to keep the laws, obey the Sabbath, avoid drinking, and peace breaking; above all to be obedient. The end result was that he would go to heaven by being morally subservient. The inconsistency, of course, is that slavery created and nurtured the vices that the slaves were admonished to flee.

For example, how do you encourage a man to be faithful to his wife when you break up his family by selling his wife to one plantation and his children to another? The afflictions of the black family even now are the continuing impacts of the patterns set by the "Christian" forefathers since the 1620's. The source of this distorted view of morality is well expressed in Joseph Washington's observation:

> In 1726, the Evangelical Revival in Europe erupted in the Great Awakening in the colonies. The spirit was that of Calvinism. Calvinism has everywhere and always lacked interest in the common man, preferring to oppose the sins of excessiveness and sensuality rather than those of inequality and injustice.[12]

3. Ample evidence abounds that many slaves were members of the same churches as their masters. They could only worship, not share in decisions or other activities as equals. Often a "slave gallery" or place at the back of the church or the side of the church was designated for them. Before and after the Civil War there is an abundance of records indicating the desire for the separation of members based on racial identity. One example follows:

> The First Baptist Church, in the city of Louisville, Kentucky, was a white congregation, now known as the Walnut Street Baptist Church. This congregation had its beginning in the year 1815, just five years after Louisville became a city. As was the custom in most southern communities, Negro slaves were admitted as members, with very

limited privileges and assigned seats in the balcony. In the year 1829, on the first Sunday in November eighteen slave members were given letters of dismission and were granted the privilege of worshipping to themselves, "under their own vine and fig tree." [13]

John Lee Eighmy says that:

> The desire for separatism did not stop with the etiquette of distinction practiced when the races worshipped together. White Baptists made perfectly clear their preference for complete separation in religious life. State conventions often studied the problem of how best to give religious instruction to the colored. One theme runs through these reports: the method most highly recommended called for separate meetings and, whenever possible, the use of separate quarters.[14]

As unfortunate as this move was for the development of authentic Christianity in America there was a side benefit for the Negro. Apart from the folk religion that developed around the church, an authentic religious expression peculiar to the Negro began to emerge. Eventually there was the blending of that which he created when he worshiped in secret with that which was received from corporate worship with other Christians. The syncretism along with later developments gave form to the peculiarity of worship in the black church.

4. Another effect which the Great Awakening had was in the development of a social consciousness against slavery. Even as great reforms against coarse popular amusements, widespread illiteracy, injustice before the courts, child labor abuse, and industrial abuse, followed the spiritual awakening in England, so did a consciousness against social amenities develop in America. The religious enthusiasm in the North gave the free and educated black a platform for his attack on slavery. He was joined by some whites, especially Quakers, who extended their influence when possible into the South.

Noticeably absent was the prominence of a concerted abolitionist movement among white Baptists and Methodists in the South. This is of interest in light of the fact that most free Negroes and slaves responded overwhelmingly to the Baptist and Methodist expressions of the Great Awakening. Because the economic support of these churches and their organizational structures depended on the slave owners, these churches and organizations were noticeably silent or negative on issues that would incite their constituency. They retreated to a major emphasis of evangelism (soul saving) piety, moralism, other worldliness. Their loyalty was clearly to "the Southern cause." Some went even so far as to sever the ties with their northern counterparts in order to maintain the status quo.

The above is not intended to negate the influence of some voices among Baptists and Methodists in the South. Some did have pangs of conscience about the evils of the slave system. John Lee Eighmy cites the following as indications of concern among Baptists in the South:

> The earliest known Baptist action on slavery occurred in 1710, when a South Carolina church questioned the cruelty of punishments allowed by the slave code. At the time of the American Revolution, many Baptists freed their slaves while churches vigorously entered into the anti-slavery debate. A Georgia association opposed future importation of slaves in 1793. Some Baptists in the Carolinas considered slavery to be incompatible with Christianity. The General Committee, representing the states' six district bodies, condemned slavery as a "violent deprivation of the rights of nature" and then advised Baptists to "make use of every legal measure to extirpate the horrid evil from our land." Slavery became an even livelier issue farther west. Some pioneer preachers in Kentucky made opposition to slavery a matter of dogma. When the regular associational bodies would not adopt an anti-slavery position, emancipationists David Barrow, Carter Tarrant and others led twelve churches to organize a separate antislavery association.[15]

These voices for abolition were few and far between. For the most part Baptists and Methodists in the South were silent, neutral, or negative to such a "divisive" issue. Some churchmen of prominence such as Richard Furman and Richard Fuller even went so far as to prepare statements supporting slavery as necessary, divinely inspired, and biblically sanctioned.

In the year 1818, Presbyterians adopted unanimously a declaration where slavery is called:

> A gross violation of the most precious of human nature, utterly inconsistent with the law of God, which requires us to love our neighbor as ourselves, and totally irreconcilable with the spirit and principles of Jesus Christ, which enjoin that "all things whatsoever ye would that men should do to you, do ye also to them." [16]

But the General Assembly still permitted slaveholders to hold office in the church, in spite of its statement concerning slavery as a gross violation of human rights. The violators were exhorted to "continue and increase their exertions to effect a total abolition of slavery, with no greater delay than a regard to the public welfare demands, and recommends that if a Christian professor shall sell a slave, who is also in communion with our church, without the consent of the slave, the seller should be suspended till he should *repent* and make reparations." [17]

Efforts to Help

In lieu of positive abolitionists activities, however, these denominations developed patterns of work intended to aid the religious development of the Negro. The history of Southern Baptists and its activities at this point is illustrative.

After the Southern Baptist Convention was organized in 1845, one of its first tasks was to plan for missionary work among blacks. The Board of Domestic Missions (now the Home Mission Board) was "instructed to take all prudent measures for the religious instruction of our colored population." Southern Baptists have continued this ministry by working with Negro Baptist churches, associations, and state conventions. They have provided institutes, extension education centers, the American Baptist Seminary, teacher missionaries, regional missionaries, scholarship assistance, and financial support for agreed-upon projects. They have underwritten the salaries for Negroes employed in denominational services of various kinds.

In the middle colonies the missionary work was led by Thomas Bray, who devised plans to convert adult blacks and to educate their children. It proved to be unsuccessful. Missionary work among blacks in Pennsylvania found less obstacles than in the other middle colonies. Blacks were baptized as early as 1712 and also shared in the worship and attended services regularly. In the colonies farther north where fewer blacks were to be found, the problem of religious indoctrination was not too prevalent.

The missionary movement received another setback with the Puritans of New England. They desired to see the blacks saved but did not want to see them connected with a state church that would give them political and religious freedom. This was a problem for the church then, and it is a problem for the church *now*.

From 1750 to 1859 the controversy over slavery found its way into the churches. The reactions of the Southern religious bodies were decidedly proslavery. In many of the predominantly white churches, the Negroes voluntarily withdrew or were forced out. Whites also withdrew from churches which were predominantly black. However, in the latter's case they were not forced to leave by blacks but by social stigma. An excellent illustration is found in the origin of the Shiloh Baptist Church of Northumberland County, Virginia. In the year 1867, thirty-eight Negroes, all members of the Fairfield Baptist Church (white) addressed the following letter to the white members:

POPLAR STAGE
July 7, 1867

To Elder William Kirk and
The members of the Fairfield Baptist Church

BELOVED BROTHERS:

Grace be unto you and peace from God, the Father of our Lord Jesus Christ. From an earnest desire to act in all things with an eye *single* to the glory of God and for the unity of that common faith which constitute us in Christ Jesus, we have thought it advisable to counsel on the subject of our future church relation. So that whatever may be done we may at least *preserve* that peace and harmony which ought to characterize those of the same faith and order and promote the prosperity of that cause which, through *your instrumentality,* had been the means of calling us into the light and knowledge of the glorious gospel of the Son of God. Without alluding to the Providence that so mysteriously changed our *social* and *political* relation, we conceive that under the *new order* of things we are not only advanced in our religious privilege, but that *solemn* and *weighty* responsibilities impose upon us a new class of *duties* in which we should be wanting in fidelity *if* we did not seek to place ourselves in that position in which we could best promote our *mutual* good, both in reference to ourselves and our posterity.

This new relation the subject of a separate church organization presses itself upon us as the *best possible way* in which we can best promote those indispensable interests, such as an ordained ministry, a separate congregation with all the privileges of a church organization, stated church meetings, regular religious service, Sabbath Schools, etc. But just at this point the question arises: Can we not do this and preserve the *unity* of the *faith* and continue in church *fellowship* with our white brethren; and thereby perpetuate our church identity, so that in all the general interest of the church we may be mutually interested and to some extent co-laborers? To effect this may require the *concurrent action* of all the members of the congregation concerned; and the object of this communication is to ask your attention to this subject with the *hope* that such an arrangement can be made as to induce a general church meeting at some convenient time and place for this purpose, that our identity may be preserved or perpetuated if possible; and if not, that we may receive your parting benediction and blessing, as well as your endorsement of our Christian Character and standing. All of which is most respectfully submitted for your prayerful consideration and action. Hoping that unerring wisdom may guide us in the way of all truth, we remain, dear brethren in the bond of Christ.

Yours Fraternally,
SAMUEL CONWAY, Secretary
HIRMAN KENNER, Chairman [18]

It is interesting to note that these people desired to carry out their wishes in the present church building, but on August 10, 1867, two white members donated small plots of land for a new church building.

The first black Baptist church is reported to have been at Silver Bluff, South Carolina, founded about 1773–75. The First Baptist Church, Savannah, Georgia, is reportedly the oldest *sustained* black congregation (1778 or 79). There was a period of time during which the Silver Bluff church did not exist.[19]

The African Methodist Episcopal Church of Philadelphia, Pennsylvania, an early black church, was founded in 1816. Its founder, Richard Allen, was born a slave of Benjamin Chew of Philadelphia. He was converted to Christianity in 1777. One of his first converts was his master. This new conversion changed his master's mind about slavery. Thus he permitted Allen and other bondsmen to obtain their freedom.

The wavering in their religious conduct by these three major bodies only delayed and did not help the churches in ultimately avoiding denominational splits which came in 1844 for the Methodists, in 1845 for the Baptists, and in 1861 for the Presbyterians.

The post-Civil War and Reconstruction periods (1866–1899) marked the beginning of phenomenal growth of the Negro churches. By the close of the Civil War, segregated galleries in white churches became mere architectural relics. As this period came to a close it found blacks who were Methodists, Baptists, Presbyterians, Congregationalists, Episcopalians, and Roman Catholics.

Since 1899

In the years since 1899 blacks have joined other religious movements and denominations. Following World Wars I and II large numbers left the South for the northern urban centers. Out of the crises and trauma of life in these new areas there arose personality cults and Pentecostal churches. The personality cults include such organizations as Father Divine's Peace Movement, Daddy Grace, and Prophet Jones. Many lesser known men continue similar "religious" movements all over the nation.

Religious personality cults have begun in response to the physical and material needs of urban subcultures. They promise "deliverance" and provide hope, for a fee. There is usually just enough of

Christian practice included to make these movements legitimate.

The Pentecostal or Holiness churches have also risen in influence and numbers in black communities in the postwar eras. These have formed out of the emotional needs of urban dwellers and the sterility and sophistication of some mainline denominations.

Blacks may be found in most other religious movements of this century including the Black Muslims, Jehovah's Witnesses, Christian Scientists, and the Unity movement.

The largest concentration of black religionists may be found in the Baptist and Methodist churches.

There are three dominant conventions of black Baptists: the National Baptist Convention of America, Inc.; the National Baptist Convention of America, Unincorporated; and the Progressive National Baptist Convention of America, Inc.

Until 1894 there were area or regional conventions and cause-oriented conventions. Sometimes the same churches supported a variety of conventions with different objectives. In 1894 a consolidation meeting was held in Montgomery, Alabama. This meeting brought together three organizations, the Foreign Mission Convention (1880), the American National Baptist Convention (1886), and the Baptist National Educational Convention (1893). These three organizations formed the National Baptist Convention of America. The purposes of foreign missions, home missions, and education were provided by boards in the new convention. The first annual session was held in Atlanta, Georgia, in 1895.

The first split in this convention came in 1897 when some, feeling that the cause of foreign missions was not receiving adequate support, formed the Lott Carey Foreign Mission Convention. This organization continues with foreign missions as its prime objective. Headquartered in Washington, D.C., the Lott Carey Convention receives its major support from several East Coast states.

The first split of a national consequence came in 1915. The issue over the ownership of the publishing house in Nashville, Tennessee, had been building for several years. After years of entangled strife over business and legal procedures those churches supporting

Dr. R. H. Boyd, the corresponding secretary of the publishing house, formed a convention using the name National Baptist Convention of America, Unincorporated. Sometimes this is referred to as the Boyd Convention. The main contingent of churches kept the same name but added "Incorporated" to their title. This was not only to distinguish themselves, but also to recognize their legal entity. This convention has been referred to by the names of its presidents, Townsend Convention (A. M. Townsend) or Jackson Convention (J. H. Jackson).

The next national split came in 1961 after a four-year battle over tenure of convention officers. Feeling the matter irreconcilable, those churches supporting tenure formed the Progressive National Baptist Convention of America, Incorporated.

These three conventions comprise a membership of more than eleven million black Christians in America. In numerical rank the Incorporated Convention is first; the Unincorporated Convention is second; and the Progressive Convention is third. Blacks may also be found in the American and Southern Baptist Conventions. Some are dually aligned in one of the National Baptist Conventions and in either the American or Southern Baptist Convention. The purpose of dual alignment has been for fellowship in the National Baptist Conventions and program in either of the others.

The Methodist churches composed the second largest group of black religious adherents. In addition to being in the predominantly white national bodies, blacks are to be found in the African Methodist Episcopal Church (1816), the African Methodist Episcopal Zion Church (1822), or the Christian (formerly Colored) Methodist Episcopal Church (1870).

The Christian faith continues to be the most unifying element in black American life. The chapters which follow will elaborate on the reasons for this.

3 • Worship in the Black Church

DEARING E. KING

There is no such thing as a "black church" or a "white church."
If you will agree with me on that, then I will agree with you and use
the terms to accommodate our abortive designations. With that
understanding, let me restate the subject—"Worship in the Black
Church."

Today when Christians are divided over most issues, there seems
to be one point of unanimous agreement: we are headed in the
wrong direction, and we are getting nowhere fast. Too long has our
American church life, based on race, been expressed in the words
of a disgusted pastor. After a stormy official board meeting, the
pastor was called upon to close the meeting with prayer. In an
atmosphere of confusion the veteran minister said: "Lord, as Thou
has blessed us in our coming together, now bless us as we come
apart." That prayer would not be amiss for our dilemma as we
gather here in a common confession that we cannot actually sing:
"We are not divided, all one body we." With that admission it is
my prayer and hope that we might turn with an openness of heart,
mind, and spirit in the right direction of togetherness.

Worship is the best place to begin. Since worship is the central
act of the church of Jesus Christ, we may well perceive the divine
judgment upon the distorted image of Christ on the American form
of Christianity. The true image of Christ has been defaced, which
makes the American church life a mere form of godliness. Therefore, this form needs to be reminted so that Christ's image might
be restored. "For the time is come," says the apostle Peter, "that
judgment must begin in the house of God" (1 Peter 4:17).

Without looking again at the scandal of separation between the races in American church life, it would be impossible to understand the uniqueness of worship in the black church. You see, worship may be defined as a spontaneous consciousness of God's presence. Hence, a public service of worship itself should be a corporate experience, a prayerful togetherness. Such an act of corporate worship takes place whenever worshipers of various backgrounds, points of view, social and individual differences assemble together to affirm their personal identities in an authentic sharing of God's presence, grace, power, will, and purpose for the betterment of their own lives and for others. When this cannot be accomplished so that our lives may level off to a common Christian brotherhood, then the left-out person or group has to seek other worship arrangements. That accounts for—"Worship in the Black Church."

Worship and Self-realization

For a meaningful understanding of worship in the black church, let us begin with the black thrust for self-realization. Because black people were locked out from the in-white-group everywhere else, they felt that their last resort was the white church, since that was the only church existing during the time of slavery. For some unknown reason, blacks could be fooled about everything else except the church of Christ. Even their white slave masters taught them that the church is a body of baptized believers in Christ. It is a community of the committed. Hence, the Negro bent over backwards in an effort to be accepted into the white church, which was the only Christian community that he knew about. But for more than three hundred years the white church has been more concerned with immunity than with community and with disaffiliation than with reconciliation. As a result, for the most part, blacks have been denied the right and privilege of participation in the white church. From slavery until now blacks have been humiliated, embarrassed, harrassed, brutally attacked, arrested, and imprisoned for even attempting to worship in white churches of all denominations. Even when they were admitted to worship and membership in a few white churches, they were relegated to the rear or to the balconies.

They were also forced to wait until whites were served the Lord's Supper before they were served.

From the treatment suffered by blacks in the white church it is, indeed, a miracle that they did not renounce Christianity altogether. Perhaps they would have if they had not, psychologically, separated Christ from the white church. Even by the simplest approach to Christian understanding, it was utterly impossible for the most insensitive to tolerate such racist, unchristian acts of worship in the house of God.

Out of that scandal of separation the black church came into being as a thrust of black people for self-realization. They asked the question with the apostle Paul: "Is Christ divided?" Their answer was in leaving the white church. That was the only way that they could be a part of the body of Christ, since they could not be in the body of Christ within the white church. Otherwise, there would have been a stunting of the moral and spiritual growth of black believers if they had remained within the dehumanizing and depersonalizing structure of white American "churchianity." Their only option for self-realization was to originate their own place of worship where they could be in the body of their living Lord. From this place developed the unique distinctions of worship in the black church.

Worship and Unwavering Faith

The basic distinction is an unwavering faith in the absolute sovereignty of the supreme, infinite Creator. This faith must have been mysteriously and miraculously delivered to black people. They could not read nor were there schools for them to attend. They had no persons or institutions to which they could look or on which they could depend for relief, religiously or legally, including the United States Government.

More strangely still was the ability of blacks to identify themselves with the Hebrews who were in similar bondage under Pharaoh in Egypt and how they had tried to liberate themselves to no avail. The Hebrews came to the point of no return. In their extremity, God revealed himself to Moses in absolute, divine sovereignty, saying:

"I have surely seen the affliction of my people which are in Egypt, and have heard their cry by reason of their taskmasters; for I know their sorrows; and I am come down to deliver them out of the hand of the Egyptians, and to bring them up out of that land unto a good land and a large, unto a land flowing with milk and honey" (Ex. 3:7–8).

This absolute sovereign power is the base of worship in the black church. In short, there is no more sublime fact in the history and experience of the black church than her steady, unwavering faith in the absolute sovereignty of God. This anchored faith in the Eternal was strangely delivered to black slaves, and they religiously transmitted it, through worship, to successive generations. From that immovable sovereign base black people have always had room enough to sing and shout from earth to heaven.

Yes, through divine providence the absolute sovereign power of God was revealed to black people among the bulrushes of the Nile River where God's chosen people had been stripped of their freedom and reduced to oppressive slavery in Egypt. There blacks established identity with the Hebrews and connected that divine sovereignty to the black plantation soil along the Mississippi River to which they had been taken from their African homeland and reduced from persons to property. There, amidst inhuman conditions and animalistic treatment, they got a glimpse of the Almighty which was revealed in a stable at Bethlehem.

That connection, from the bulrushes on the Nile River to the little Jesus boy, born in a manger, has been the sovereign key by which black people have entered humble places of worship and built altars as they lifted their voices with David in this psalm of praise: "The earth is the Lord's, and the fulness thereof; the world, and they that dwell therein." Or, as Deacon Terry Rogers used to pray: "From everlasting to everlasting; from way back beyond back; before there was a when or a where, or a then or a there; you stepped out from nowhere and stood on nothing, and said, Let there be; and worlds leaped from your presence like sparks from a blacksmith's anvil. Then you left word that whenever I needed you to call you. Lord,

I need you now because I have no one else to turn to." After Brother Rogers' prayer the choir would march in singing: "Holy! Holy! Holy! there is none beside Thee." The pastor always closed the worship with this benediction: "Now unto the only wise God, our Father."

This unwavering faith in the absolute sovereignty of the supreme, infinite Creator is the key to worship in the black church. Because black people have been cramped into oppressive social structual confinement, their very existence demanded that they would give their devotion to the sovereign Supreme Being outside of themselves. When black people meet to worship their sovereign Lord, it is because they know through faith that only he could unify their disconnected, disorganized, and fragmented existence.

Worship and Spiritual Creativity

Another distinction of worship in the black church is spiritual creativity. Here we see worship in the black church as a contradistinction to worship in white churches. The very use of the terms "the white church" and "the black church" is an obvious admission that the church has practiced birth control; and in the process it has become spiritually uncreative and unproductive. In the very nature of the church of Christ, the purpose of authentic worship is to bring worshipers into a conscious relationship with God, and into a spiritual relationship with all believers in Christ. Hence, through the ministry of worship, people may be directed in their quest for the reality of God and for the fellowship of kindred minds as "like to that above." This is a spiritually creative experience in the black church for her worship deals primarily with the only two realities, God and people—all people. Thus, a spiritual, social fellowship edifies common humanity. For these reasons true worship reaches its highest expression in mutual group sharing.

For instance, black people have always realized that there can be no genuine worship experience based upon the sovereign power of God alone. Authentic worship in the church of Jesus Christ must include both God and neighbor. This is mandatory, not only for spiritual creativity in the life of the church, but for the inheritance of eternal life for each believer in Christ. This is what the parable of the good Samaritan is all about. The activities of the Jewish priest and Levite were about religion; while the spiritual creativity of the good Samaritan was about life. This is the reason why new, creative life was generated in the man who had fallen among thieves and was stripped, beaten, and left half dead.

The reason why spiritual creativity is noticeable in worship in the black church is because worshipers are actually involved with God and neighbor. From its inception the black church has had no policy denying either membership or seating to people because of skin color, creed, or station in life. Without the involvement of both God and neighbor, no institution or organization can even be labeled as the church of Jesus Christ.

Because worship in the black church involves both God and neighbor, there is a freedom of expression and movement that is not of this world. This enables black congregations to transcend time, place, and conditions. A white pastor said to a black pastor: "Why do you hold services so long?" The black pastor answered: "We wait until the Holy Spirit comes. But you miss the Holy Spirit because you spend more time getting out of church than you do getting in."

Worship in the black church is not subject to any rigid rule of order. The main features of the service are singing, praying, preaching, and giving. In many instances much time is taken for announcements. This is necessary because the black church through its spiritual creativity gave birth to many black organizations, businesses, and movements. Therefore, time has to be allowed to promote the work of such agencies as the NAACP, the Urban League, the Southern Christian Leadership Conference, black newspapers, and so forth. These agencies have fought the Negro's cause when the white church and the Federal Government failed to do so.

No church has experienced music, instrumentally and otherwise, as is creatively rendered in the black church. Listen, if you please, to a Negro organist or pianist, and you will agree that he is creatively reaching for the lost chord. He plays people into breathless ecstasy. Listen to the singing. Musicians and singers creatively improvise, composing something brand new out of old tunes. They may sing a song through for two or three times and repeat the refrain indefinitely without conveying a sense of routine or boredom. Often, they make up songs and tunes on the spot. That is spiritual creativity of the first magnitude.

Without question, preaching in the black church is the main feature of worship. There is absolutely nothing in heaven or on earth like a black preacher. And if he is a Baptist preacher, you may double the dose. His contribution to black people in particular and to America in general can never be adequately appraised. He has literally stood with the prophet Ezekiel in the valley of dry bones with an optimism and a gospel of hope that must be the mystery that angels desire to look into. He is not a reciter of nothings, moving his head around a collar turned hind-parts-before. When he stands up to preach, he is involved in reinacting the divine act of redemption.

For instance, when black slaves were not allowed to congregate or to communicate in groups, the Negro preacher, who had to keep his identity as a preacher concealed, devised ways of preaching to the slaves. He would tell the water boy to announce the service at a given time by singing through the fields: "Steal Away." All of the slaves knew to go to the swampy forest that night for worship. Another slave would be stationed at the big house to ascertain whether or not the acts of worship could be heard. The next morning he went through the fields singing: "O, I couldn't hear nobody pray."

When the slave preacher gave such a vivid description of Christ, his birth, his life, his death, resurrection, and ascension, the Negroes knew that he could not read; so they asked him in the words of the spiritual: "Were you there when they crucified my Lord?"

Take for example, the late John Jasper of old Sixth Mt. Zion Church of Richmond, Virginia. It is said that on one Easter Sunday morning, he was preaching and demonstrating how Jesus raised

Lazarus from the grave. In the balcony was a white student from the Richmond Union Seminary with his son. John Jasper created an almost visible grave as he had Jesus bring Lazarus forth. Several times he said, "Jesus said to Lazarus, 'Come forth.' " The student's little boy said: "Daddy, come on, let's go." The student and the congregation were transfixed as Jasper had Jesus bring Lazarus forth. Finally, the son got up and said, "Daddy, let's go before he makes the man get up." That is spiritual creativity when a preacher is able to raise the dead on Sunday morning.

The creative, reinactment of the divine act of redemption has brought about the most unique and effective ministry in the world. Through preaching, black preachers have vindicated the faith which Christ pledged in them by giving them a place when they and their people were left out of the existing church life. Certainly, Christ must repeat himself as he sees black preachers lifting congregations from despair, sin, and death as he said to the seventy and two: "I beheld Satan as lightning fall from heaven" (Luke 10:18).

Through the spiritual creativity of worship in the black church, blacks can boast with John that "now we are the sons of God, and it doth not yet appear what we shall be."

Worship as Celebration

This brings us to the final distinction of worship in the Black Church. It is the act of celebration. This call to celebration is with such unrehearsed and undirected joyful enthusiasm that it has amazed all other churches looking in from the outside. What is it, you ask, that makes black people so joyful, so supremely happy? Why do they make so much noise over Christ and their newfound joy in their Lord? What is it that holds them in church all day on Sunday from week to week?

Black congregations meet to celebrate the sovereignty of God. When you see them falling into one another's arms and shouting "Glory Hallelujah," they are not exercising any more than the children of Israel did when God led them through the Red Sea. That was no time to be quiet. It was time to celebrate; so they broke out with a shout: "The Lord is my strength and song, and he is become my salvation: . . . The Lord is a man of war: the Lord is his name" (Ex. 15:2–3). The triumphant entry of Jesus to Jerusalem to announce his reign as King did not inspire frozen silence. It was a call to celebration, and "the multitudes that went before, and that followed, cried, saying, Hosanna to the son of David: Blessed is he that cometh in the name of the Lord; Hosanna in the highest" (Matt. 21:9).

Or take this triumphant note of praise when God had wrought a great victory for black people, they spontaneously sang: "Ride on King Jesus, no man can hinder you."

This celebration in worship is at the heart of the black church, for it is the only act of worship that no other body claims or attempts in the black tradition and manner.

In the black church, worship is fundamentally the only important service of the week; for people meet to celebrate the sovereignty of God for what he is, for what he has done and is doing for them, and in gratitude for Christ in pledging his faith in them as his children. In the celebration they also meet to renew their pledge and commitment to him.

They also meet to celebrate because the black church is a survival institution where all people may come into an open door that no man can shut. There was a time when black people could not enter through the doors of education, politics, and other fields, but there has always been the door of revelation open to them. Perhaps no other race or people in the Christian era has shared John's position on the Isle of Patmos more than black people. As you know, when the door of revelation was open to John, the Isle of Patmos was no longer a desolate uninhabitable place. As a matter of fact, John did not even acknowledge it as a place. He says: "I was in the isle that is called Patmos."

For nearly the past twenty years, Negroes had similar experiences. Their thrust for self-realization in equality and justice in the total economy of this nation exposed them to the most vicious atrocities ever suffered by a people. But through the doors of black churches and thank God, a few white churches, all people, black, white, red, and polka-dot participated in sit-ins, wade-ins, march-ins, and jail-ins. For the first time in American history, Dr. Martin Luther King, Jr., led people through blood, tears, and even death out of the fear of police and imprisonment. It was merely an isle that was called Patmos. This called for celebration even at the funeral of Dr. King.

No other people have withstood so much for so long. It is, indeed, a great tribute to the black church that black people have been able to survive. Even the waiting has been a source of celebration.

The genius of the black church has been in its ability to accelerate time by celebrating things hoped for, the evidence of things not seen. Although Abraham did not actually see the realization of his desire as a fact, Jesus says: "Abraham desired to see this day, and he saw it." Through worship, Negroes have always been able to celebrate their potential as a reality. Dr. Martin Luther King, Jr., said that when he boarded a segregated bus in Atlanta, Georgia, before he would take a seat in the rear, assigned to blacks, he would always make his mind sit on the front seat. That was celebration of things hoped for. For instance, in worship blacks have always known that the day would come when this nation would have black mayors, black congressmen, black senators, black sheriffs, black judges, and so forth.

I remember a sermon preached by Reverend Petsy Brown when I was about seven years old. When he got through describing what we shall be, my mother pulled me into her arms and said: "Mamma's little boy is going to be President of these United States." You see, we do not celebrate what has happened; we celebrate our potential. This always keeps us on tiptoe to announce the wondrous surprise of what is to be and to redress the balance of the past. In worship, for blacks, the future has always infringed upon the present. Therefore, we know that it is a present now and that it can only be shared when it is celebrated.

In worship, blacks actually embrace the Kingdom, which is Christ invisibily present in his church. There they know that they live in a kingdom that is not of this world. Like the Jews, who constituted the wheel in the middle of the big Babylonian wheel, blacks constitute the wheel in the big American wheel. But unlike the Jews, who could not sing the Lord's song in a strange land, Negroes can sing, pray, preach, and give to celebrate their victory that overcomes the world.

We do not celebrate, however, as an end in itself. Our goal is Christ himself who loved us and gave himself for us. I think Dr. Raymond Henderson sums this up for us. One day he was preparing a sermon at the end of a hallway. His son kept coming down to the end of the hall; and although he said nothing, his presence was annoying. Twice he gave the boy money to go out and get candy or something from the store, but each time the boy would return and stand near his desk. Finally Dr. Henderson said, "Billy, tell me what do you want." Billy's simple reply was: "Nothing! I just want to be near you."

Worship in the Negro church is like that. We do not assemble to air the grievances of the scandal of separation or the atrocities in the past. We meet to reaffirm our undiminished faith in the absolute sovereignty of the supreme, infinite Creator "who is able to keep us from falling, and to present us faultless before the presence of his glory with exceeding joy." We must as witnesses of our own spiritual creative originality and productivity. We meet and worship because it is time to celebrate, not only because of the things that are come to pass, but because of the things that are to come. We celebrate because we know that the time will come when Baptists everywhere will drop the color bar and we shall sing: "All one body we, One in hope and doctrine, One in charity." Then once more the morning stars shall sing together and the sons of God shall shout for joy.

4·Black Preaching

HENRY H. MITCHELL

I begin by setting my topic in context. In other words, I must not attempt to start on the whole subject of black preaching in a vacuum. We must know how the subject relates to white Southern Baptist preaching tradition and to the Christian tradition in general. Or at least we must understand how I *think* they are related—what are my own basic assumptions. The presentation will hinge on these, and whatever I say can only be understood in their light.

Concerning white Southern Baptist preaching as related to black preaching, may I share an experience? It was about thirty years ago that some of my new found Union Seminary schoolmates and I sat down and did a mental survey of the great preachers of New York City, Philadelphia, and so forth. In our youthful but, as we thought of it, great wisdom, we decided that practically all of them came either from British possessions or from the American South. There was Buttrick from Scotland and Joseph Fort Newton from the South, and so on.

In due season we were moved to a consideration of why this was so. The guesses were many and varied. As I remember it, the two most impressive hypotheses were something like this. One had to do with poetry of the soul, a quality employing language, rhetoric, and so on, but perhaps best described as an impressive fusion of spiritual sensitivity and stimulating scholarship. It was a quality which we agreed was all too often squelched or never even born in the industrial centers of the North.

The other explanation was even harder to phrase—let's call it dramatic involvement. Other terms would include less inhibited expression of the total person, warmth, or liberty in the spirit.

Interestingly enough, this mostly white group of students seemed to think that this strength of Southern preaching may have stemmed from the large black presence and its influence on the culture of the South.

Whatever the validity of our impressions at that time, I have said all that to indicate that I have all these years held the clear assumption that Southern Baptist preaching has much more in common with American black preaching than any other white preaching in the United States. I also still tend to feel that this is one of the reasons that the best known revival preacher in America and many other pulpit powers are, in fact, Southern Baptists. I also have a long standing conviction that *if* this power were to be focused, with all possible intensity and spiritual creativity, on the racial evils of the South and the nation, the South would easily assume the lead over the North in the whole field of brotherhood. In fact, I believe that for this and other reasons, the South could quite plausibly be the first area of our nation to solve outright the problems arising from centuries of white oppression and prejudice.

This reminds me of another incident, which took place fifteen or more years ago. I was serving as assistant to a white American Baptist executive whose original home had been Texas. I had heard that he had paid a visit to Southern Baptist general headquarters in Nashville, after attending an executive meeting in St. Louis. In my typically frank way, I wanted to know what he was doing at "enemy" headquarters and at whose expense did he go. The answer he gave, as we drove down the highway, will always ring in my soul. It was not long after the Supreme Court decision desegregating the schools, and he had gone to Nashville to try to convince some of his old friends in high office there of their strategic place in the spiritual history of the world. You see, he agreed with me that the greatest need in the Southern Baptist pulpit was a world-shaking goal like maybe brotherhood. He was also certain that if they would tackle it, the greatest revival in world history would break out. The irony of it was that many of the men he approached heartily agreed with him. They said, some with tears in their eyes, that they wished they had the faith to try, or they wished they had a greater sense that this was an idea whose time had come. My dear friend, the white executive from Texas, was surely not ahead of God's will, but he was far ahead of his fellow Southerners.

However, I am sure there can be no doubt, now, that the time has indeed come for all-out justice, brotherhood, and all that this may cost all of us in reordered priorities. And I suppose also that I have no right to hide my conviction that the best of your preaching could, with a proper acceptance of this mandate from heaven, set the South and the world on fire. I have this confidence partly because the best of Southern Baptist preaching is surely kin to the best of black preaching. They were born, for the most part, in the same place and at some of the same times, and they have lived side by side all these years. The black tradition went North and West sooner, but they are even following the same pattern of diaspora. The relationship between us, regardless of the horrible atrocities, is, in form and often in substance, the closest relationship we black preachers have outside the black world.

Black Preaching and the Total Christian Tradition

The relationship to the total Christian tradition is less known in depth, and much more subtle. Even to state the relationship one has to establish first an understanding concerning basic Christianity as opposed to the widely prevalent white Western version. May I therefore briefly describe this contrast first?

The gospel was, as Paul said, foolishness (1 Cor. 1:23) to Greeks. It was not intellectually systematic. Today we would say that it was "primitive." Paul was aware that this was no recommendation in Greek culture, and so he proceeded to remedy the erstwhile flaw, despite his protestations to the contrary. He made his words to Greeks about Christ and the cross as cogent and systematic as possible. He moved so far in the direction of Greek culture as to quote a Stoic pantheist thought by some to be Epimenides. He said, "For in him we live, and move, and have our being; as certain also of your own [Greek] poets have said" (Acts 17:28). He was *entering* their culture and building on their strengths. It never dawned on him to destroy or ignore so important a part of their lives. The result was that this Stoic pantheist quotation is now a part of our Holy Bible. And why not?

This inevitable and legitimate process of cultural entrance and adaptation was continued when Christianity was carried to northern Europe. This time it was so-called "pagan" festivals that were baptized into the faith, just as these Greek sayings had been and as some other Greek religious practices had been baptized into the faith. The result was a Christianity now widely known for winter festivals with "Christmas trees," and spring festivals with "Easter eggs," and a calendar with days like Sunday and Thursday, all of these clearly indicating "pagan" objects and styles of worship.

I have no quarrel with any of this. The problem is simply that when Christianity was carried to other continents this same cultural adaptability ceased. Thus, European holidays, attire, language, and customs were declared to be *the* definitive "Christianity." This was cultural imperialism and violence of the worst sort, and all over the world people are more and more aware of it. Not only did it destroy the people thus belittled, and not only did it destroy the full impact of Christ on them and their culture, it also impoverished the gospel itself by robbing it of the enrichment that has come every time the faith has had genuine dialogue with any culture. When Paul reached out towards the Greeks, he capitalized on their strengths and thus enriched Christianity as a *whole*. In so doing he helped to give the gospel the greatest adaptability, perhaps, of any world religion in the facing of the modern intellectual revolution, the age of science, the cause-and-effect world view.

My quarrel has to do with the fact that there are other challenges to be faced by the gospel, and other cultures with other strengths to be used of God in the facing of those problems. We *need* desperately, today, what God could do for all men through these cultures and their interpretation of his word. But white arrogance has caused missionaries and others to assume that white Western culture, much like the Bible, was *the culture* once and for all delivered to the saints.

I feel especially keenly about this because black Christianity and black preaching have thus been considered outside the accepted and "orthodox" mainstream of where God is at work in the world. Thus, when whites begin losing their youth and facing other weaknesses in their faith, they have carefully avoided black models in their search for answers. They have tried coffeehouses, guitars and drums, so-called "dialogue," and so-called "celebration." Man, we've been doing that stuff for over two hundred years. But nobody seems willing to search all-out for the ways in which such factors have been used in black religion, not as instant culture gimmicks but time-honored aspects of a highly developed religion and culture.

I have real questions about people who go out and suddenly "make" a culture or a style of worship. These things have to come with long rootage in human experiences. If they want dialogue with old roots, we've got it. If they want to know what celebration is all about, that's all we ever did. We did that before we heard about Jesus. Thus, despite the sometimes close kinship, nobody has set out seriously to study the black pulpit for the saving inputs it might offer the white pulpit. It's fine for the best of black preachers to skim cream off the best of two worlds, but whites all too often seem determined to settle for the narrow impoverishment of only one culture.

All of this is designed to say only two things about black Christianity and its relationship to Christianity as a whole: (1) Our black fathers did in fact engage in their own independent adaptation of Christianity to their African culture and the traditional religions which dominated it. (2) The result has been a very powerful and relevant black Christianity, when seen at its best. Whatever blacks do that is different from what whites do—whatever we have kept of our African heritage—is at *least* as legitimate as Christmas trees and Easter eggs. It may in some ways be even more faithful to the original primitive Christianity, which was started as oral tradition in a culture quite similar to West African and several other so-called "primitive" cultures. The fact that it deals therefore with the still primitive feelings of all mankind, while integrating into itself the wisdom of the intellectual revolution, makes black religion and especially black preaching at their best a very possibly chosen instrument or vessel of God for these perilous days. It would be difficult to conceal my conviction that this is so.

One other area of understanding must be established. It has to do with the designation of *which* of the many facets of black preaching I shall be thinking of when I use the term. First, let me repeat that I shall be thinking of the best, the most soundly biblical and practically relevant preaching, as well as the most inspired and creative. I seek models for inspiration and guidance, not targets for criticism. Like the "white folks," I study the *successes* rather than the failures.

I also speak primarily of that which reaches the vast majority of blacks. The wide spectrum of black preaching includes varying degrees of traditional African influence and modern American black rural and urban ghetto influence. But all of these varieties are one in their attempts to keep alive and to liberate an oppressed people. Formal education and social and economic status vary, however, causing variety in black preaching utterance. Threads of the single experience run through them all, but if I seem to speak more of that variety which reaches the black masses, it may be because the threads are more obvious there.

I make this statement simply because I want it understood that while there are other folks besides Baptists, Pentecostals, and a few Methodists, I speak of them because this is where the types are and where the typology shows itself more clearly. Some of my friends seem to think that I am trying to wish the Presbyterians and Episcopalians and all such people out of business, but that just isn't so. I only want them to come home culturally. I don't care what denominational label they have, if they preach with the conviction of our black fathers, somebody will be saved.

A History of Black Religion

Let us now turn to a survey of black preaching itself, much of which is contained in my book by the same name. As I talk about black preaching, I am aware of continuing resistance to the idea that we are different, but I am strongly inclined to believe we are and glad of it. We must then look for the historical roots of black preaching and black religion. This is necessary to legitimize our faith and our utterance in the minds of a great many militants—so called— who insist on saying: "Black religion was something white folks gave us; a game they ran on us to make us docile and pliable, to make us good servants who would work hard with no complaints."

Let me say, first of all, for the longest time the white man *didn't want* us to become Christians. In fact, he didn't want to admit we had a soul. From 1619 when the first slaves landed until 1773 there was no black church anywhere, only blacks in white church galleries. For 150, even 200 years blacks had no concentrated exposure to Christianity. During that period of time all sorts of blacks became Christian, and very often became Christian because they *wanted to* and not because anybody was trying to teach them. To be sure, there were people who did teach. For example, at my wife's home in South Carolina the Episcopalians started out bright and early (1695) teaching us to read so that we could study the catechism. Some of the most dangerous people, from the white man's view of his ability to dominate blacks, came out of South Carolina, because they taught those rascals to read "too quick." South Carolina continued even through 1920 to be the capital of black intellectual production for church leaders.

Apart from these few exceptions the vast majority of blacks had to "steal" their Christian faith by listening to what was said to others. In the process they only slowly came to be what we now know as Christians, but they were still *often* ahead of their masters. This accounts for men like Richard Allen, who was said to have led his master to conversion, and not vice versa.

In that period they picked up bits and snatches which meshed with their original African traditional religion. In other words nobody had to sell them a bill of goods. Nobody had to press them. The religion they had when they came here was quite compatible with

Christianity. Since they were from many African languages they had to talk about their religion in English, which means that it had a Christian set of terms very likely before they had a legitimate standing in what we call Christian orthodox religion.

Miles Mark Fisher in his *Negro Slave Songs in the United States* quotes a report written in the nineteenth century on a preaching exercise in a camp meeting where a black brother was preaching to some of his folk. He had on a strange set of clothes, which was quite common, because blacks always believed when you were going to religious observance you ought to have the "best" of everything. So if he had on a full-dress formal, with tails flying, that was what he believed he was supposed to be wearing according to his African understanding of worship.

The report goes on to say that the gestures, the sounds, and the words he was saying were "a very strange way to address the deity." Whether whites understood him or not, it is undeniable that over this period of 150 years blacks were little by little shaping their own Christianity and using it in ways familiar to them. When they finally became what we would call thoroughbred "orthodox" Christians, they still had a great deal of the styles, movements, and expressions of their original traditional religion. Some of the things we call "country" and "ignorant"—some of the things that happened in cotton-patch churches—are in fact direct descendants of the worship you can still see in traditional religion in Africa today.

I have had Africans to tell me that when they came to the United States and sat in a Baptist church, the words were different, the songs were different, but the movements and all sorts of other things were the same as traditional (not Christian) worship. Though they didn't understand what was going on, they felt very much at home. Having been in traditional worship in Africa, I can say the same thing. There is such a remarkable kinship between traditional African religion and what we practice today that whatever is really rich about black religion when compared with white religion is the *African* enrichment, comparable to the enrichment of Christianity which Paul gave when he tried to adjust it to the *Greek* culture.

When we are different, therefore, let it be understood that we have good reason for being so, and that what we have that is different must not be destroyed. We must quit deciding that going to seminary is to change us to sound like white folks. My position—my job as black church studies professor—is to make sure we do not lose these characteristics. Now I'll wax intellectual in my classes and talk about all of those big theological terms. But I want to be sure that when those fellows go out with all of those terms in the back of their heads, and when they get ready to talk to "Aunt Jane," they will not be speaking a foreign language.

I am thoroughly convinced that what happened to our forefathers is that they were acculturated in some way to pick the best of two worlds. But when you talk of an absolutely "converted" African, I question this. They already had such strong character, such unselfish values. They had all sorts of things that were so completely Christian that missionaries in many cases have sold us a terrible bill of goods when they talked about those "pagans" bowing down to wood and stone.

I was doing some research over there recently and I sent a lady out in the streets to interview people. She found person after person from traditional villages who could quote more Bible and more African proverbs, too, which often sounded the same, than you will find from anybody here who has been through all of the American Sunday Schools. And it is so deeply ingrained in the culture that they don't know *when* they learned it.

African traditional religion and African culture is very strong. There is no problem in preparing for Christian faith, for even Jesus is prepared for by a great deal of what they believe.

Having said all of this, many scholars now believe that what happened during the "hidden years" (1623–1775) is what I refer to in my book as the emergence of the "black fathers." Their Christianity was now accepted, or black Christianity was "adequately Christian" or "legitimate." They had all of these years been developing the *fusion* between African religion and culture, and Christianity. What they did at that point began immediately to be seen as a tremendously powerful black Christian witness.

One can read the writings of a British traveler by the name of Charles Lyell who attended a service where Andrew Marshall was preaching in the First African Baptist Church of Savannah. Marshall became pastor of that church in 1812. This Britisher writes, "I never dreamed I'd find such worship among blacks." This, incidentally, can be found in a documentary history of blacks that has been published by two men named Fishel and Quarles. This British traveler says this church had a huge congregation. The pastor preached a very, very intelligent sermon on "The Eagle Stirs Her Nest." He said "the man used the animals [as African culture does], to teach many lessons." It is very likely that he picked the eagle out of the Bible because Africans talk about birds and animals to tell their children all of the lessons they need to know. When he "lapsed" into black English, into their dialect, it was very obvious that he was doing so to increase the impact of his point, and not because he suddenly waxed "ignorant" and went to speaking the black folks' language.

All of this seems clearly to document that at the beginning of the nineteenth century this fusion had taken place, to the extent that all over the colonies where black people were, there was this same kind of powerful utterance which people without any training were guided and blessed by God to develop. When I say "without any training," I guess I should reverse that and acknowledge what is really the learning process. I have already done this and indicated it in my book, *Black Preaching*.

Training of the Black Preacher

This same pastor Andrew Marshall did in fact have opportunities for learning. His use of language indicates the white part, and his handling of the eagle narrative indicates the African or black part. He and his successors did receive a form of "training," and the way the church reports it in its own documentary history is almost by accident. They were bragging about the fact that the first pastor was a body servant. This means that he was not a field hand, but was in the house and was constantly exposed to "standard" English language, reading, writing, and so forth. Thus, he became fluent and was, on the basis of this educational process, able to lead a great church. Andrew Marshall went on a little further in his exposure. The process for each pastor moves on further, so that the last "untrained" person in terms of formal education was a man who had been a body servant and had *gone to Europe* with his master. These leaders were determined to learn and to pick up the technicalities of white culture so they could go back and lead their folk. Here was a man who had been to Europe as a servant and was a great leader on the basis of this kind of education coupled with his black understandings.

Their first formally educated pastor was a man who finished Morehouse. He came in 1885, having finished in one of the earlier classes. I think of my own home church pastor (obviously before my time), a man by the name of Poindexter about whom Carter Woodson talks a great deal. Poindexter got his education as a *barber* across the street from the statehouse at Columbus, Ohio. He was pastor of the Second Baptist Church for some forty-odd years. He held high political office. He was elected to the office. He was obviously a very intelligent, first-rate leader. But the education that he got was received while people thought he was cutting their hair, as he was "picking their brains."

When we look at the "black fathers," we are *compelled* to ask, How did they become so sharp? How could they do the tremendous work they did during Reconstruction, when black preachers launched black businesses, black education, black churches, stabilized black families, and did a fantastic piece of work in government? The golden age of the black church was the Reconstruction Period and it was the golden age because of the tremendous heights to which black preachers rose both as preachers and as leaders.

When you look at all of this and wonder how, the only explanation is that they went to and fro upon the earth picking up what they could find everywhere they could find it. Even though I am a professor in a well-known seminary, I suspect that a man who would be willing, as methodically as those men did, to study everything he saw, could become just as educated as they did.

However, the fact of our time is that people who don't go to school to get what they need usually won't get it anywhere else either. So I have to suggest that most of the men go on to accredited schools today.

When I talk about the "black fathers," the great preachers, I am talking about men who learned what they did—about the Bible, about life, and about all the various disciplines which men such as Poindexter acquired—by listening to everything they heard, reading what they could find, and putting it together. That sort of thing may culminate in a kind of evolution in succeeding generations. Martin Luther King had all of the degrees including the Ph.D., but he kept the same kind of style and culture orientation that his preacher father and grandfather had. His power did not arise from his education in white schools, but despite his education and because he stood solidly in the tradition of his "black fathers," who held on to the best of their African heritage and culled the best of the white heritage, fusing them to develop what we know of as the black pulpit.

Beliefs of Black Preachers

Now I must tell what these men believed by way of doctrinal expression. Blacks took the bible very seriously, and for reasons easily traceable to their African roots. In their African roots they had known huge quantities of memorized material. Even now, the history, which is still more sung than written, is known by anybody. In one of the festivals if the performer makes one mistake, at least 200 people will say, "Whoa, go back." I mention this because even though many of these men were illiterate they came out of a culture where people (IFa priests) *memorized* thousands of proverbs.

In the Yoruba religion they have sixteen odus. Each odu has two hundred proverbs or stories, so that some of those Yoruba priests may know about as much verbatim as we have in the whole Bible. When you go to them for leadership, guidance, or divination, these men can call it right up. This explains to a large extent the way in which blacks adapted themselves to the Bible. The Bible was largely reflecting the kind of culture out of which they came. The Old Testament was so much like their culture with veneration for their fathers, etc., that some of the white missionaries hid the Old Testament. Had they shown those fellows the Old Testament, they would have said: "So what's new? Who needs it? We've got that already."

The Bible in the American black tradition quickly grew to huge importance and achieved the same kind of standing in their thinking that the old African proverbs had done. While you may say, "They were two, three, or four generations removed from that," the fact is that all of this cultural orientation continued. The *only* way you wipe out the culture and the world view or any other view that goes with it is to wipe out *people*.

Those who maintain the idea that blacks lost their culture may be right when they talk about some minor things, but in the important things like religion we've kept a whole lot more than most people think. You can see this when you look at the way blacks use the Bible. Blacks took the Bible, but not in the rigid Western sense. Their proverbs and their holy writings, or whatever you wish to call them, were used much more flexibly than the hidebound literalism that prevails among many who live in the United States.

I might suggest that what blacks have done with the Bible has been to keep all of the strengths of the so-called primitive approach to the Bible, while at the same time absorbing and integrating the intellectual world view we now have, without letting it kill the religion. So blacks are not literalistic. A few are of course, but there is nowhere near the same kind of approach to the Bible. The result has been that the average black audience would not listen to a preacher for five minutes if he didn't take a text. I know many people preach textless now, and they tell you at the seminary that you don't necessarily have to have a text. Maybe that is so with some folk, but "Man don't you be going to no black church talkin' 'bout 'My topic . . .' "

This is a tremendous strength. It is one of the things that has made the black pulpit and church as strong as it is today. The kinds of doctrinal positions that the Bible suggests, again, have been taken very seriously; but not with the rigidity that makes people go to such extremes, like they call them in the intellectual world, *reductio ad absurdum*. We don't just take an idea and force it to the point where it drives everyone crazy and is completely out of touch with reality.

The black pulpit has been much more concerned therefore with experience, with relevance. The black preacher preaches to a point, and he is very willing, as were Martin Luther King and all of his forebears, to deal with politics and any other thing that had to be dealt with. They were fully aware that all just concerns are a part of the very will of God and his kingdom. While the black preacher is a Bible-centered preacher, he is also a very life-oriented preacher.

This kind of a stance has kept the black pulpit very lively. I can still take you to places where people come early hoping to get a seat in a three thousand-seat auditorium, because somebody is proclaiming the Word in this same tradition of these "black fathers."

Let me say one other thing about the intellectual and doctrinal stance of the black pulpit. The black pulpit has not been hobbled by this whole crisis between science and reason on the one hand, and faith on the other. The black pulpit in its concern for life takes the supernatural very much in stride. We believe in folks getting healed. Blacks include the healing of the mind, body, and anything else in their traditional religion. This is not amiss, as the head of a section of the World Health Organization affirms the relationship between the health of the soul and mind that of the body (T. E. Lambo, M.D.). He indicates that the psychiatric effectiveness of traditional religion at many points has been better than that of his clinical staff of psychiatrists in Western Nigeria.

I am not trying to do away with the use of psychiatrists. I am only saying that the supernatural is very real in the black pulpit. It has not succumbed to the idea that you have to know all of the *causes* for everything. If that were the case, you would have to do away with life, for we still don't know how it is caused if you do away with the idea of God as Creator of life and the universe.

Black Preaching Style

Let me now address attention to the matter of style in the black pulpit. This is one of the more crucial issues once one has looked at the historical and doctrinal base of the black pulpit. Style has to do with the kind of colorful utterance and mannerisms, etc., that we have come to associate with the black pulpit.

The first thing has to do with freedom. The black pulpit has assumed a certain openness and permissiveness that makes it possible for a person to do almost anything he wants to if he does it sincerely. Some of you know my dear friend who pops his suspenders. Some of you know another man who says "Bless my bones"; and all of this. Nobody worries about these things because they are a part of each one's flavor as a person. He is not somebody who went somewhere and was told that you have to stick your finger up at a particular time and raise your voice at a certain point. He does it *his* way and lets *God* use him.

While there is a sense in which this occurs in other traditions, there is no doubt that the colorfulness of the black pulpit is one of the reasons why people still go long distances to hear the black preacher preach. This is also symbolically important because black people live in a world where there is no freedom. Even today, there is far less freedom than the average white mind can even imagine. On some occasions when white friends have been rather fully exposed to how completely limited the black world was, it has brought them to the verge of a nervous breakdown. The guilt feelings can be so bad that many white folks ought not to know how bad it really is, because they might not be able to take it.

The black pulpit is symbolically a place where people burst out of the bounds that have shackled them all week and are *literally free.* These *worshipers share vicariously* in the freedom of the preacher, to the extent that he does just what he feels like doing. They enjoy this.

I have a suspicion that other preachers could share this freedom if they could buck the tradition of detailed planning in worship. The average liturgical church follows right straight down the line. Everything has to conform. When you want to prove to people that you are very intelligent and educated, you follow these forms. Then, of course, you are safe. The black preacher has to be willing to take the risks to be what he is and assume that God will use it in a way that is creditable both to the Kingdom enterprise and to the preacher. It's a harder way but much better. The freedom in the pulpit is symbolic of the freedom all men must have, and it is much more effective in the way it speaks to the condition of people.

One of the more technical aspects of black preaching is the whole language which is used. I asked a friend of mine to write the foreword for my book on *Black Preaching*. He finally decided that he couldn't do it because he couldn't take the chapter on black language. The reason for this is very simple. He opposed a reality: language is a status signal. He didn't like the idea that when you talk to us you ought to sound the way *we* sound. I suppose the most profound thing that was said in the whole book was that when you quote God you ought to quote him in the native tongue. Language is a symbol. It is a sign. It tells people who you are. Now, I don't *look* very black. Some times people say, "O Lord! Here's a white man. I *know* he can't preach." But the minute "Ah gits up an starts to talkin'. . . ," (extreme to dramatize a point) the atmosphere changes. Some people come afterwards to say, "When I saw you up in the pulpit I said, 'O Lord! We ain't goin' to get a drop this mornin'.' But the minute you opened your mouth, I knowed who you was." Why, you see, that's just what I *wanted* them to know. The ear image takes precedence over the eye image. Any time you can *sound* like folk, you can reach them regardless of what you *look* like.

If I am quoting God, I don't want him to sound like somebody else. You see, this whole business of a black Christ is very important. A Warner Sallman can paint a *white* Christ (and Jesus Christ *sure* didn't look like that sissy-looking man). Then I can paint a *black* Christ, for he was at least my color or darker. Just as *visual* images must conform to the people, to diminish the distance between those people and their God, so must the *ear* images conform. People must hear God in speech that contrasts with their speech so little that they feel "he's one of us."

I have on many occasions carefully prearranged to speak the words of God, not in the so-called proper, "standard" dialect of the middle-class white, to indicate that God is one of *us*. For example, when I speak about Peter in the vision where God told him, "Rise, Peter, slay and eat," and Peter said, "What? Lord, I've *never* let anything like that touch *my* lips, *nothin'* common and dirty." Instead of having God speak in the "proper" white dialect, I say, "Looka here, Peter, don't you call nothin' *Ah* made unclean." This is the way a man would say it in black English.

If we want God to be real to black people, linguistics must also be used to present a picture of a God to whom they can relate. We are not yet in a world where people are linguistically any one thing. There is no universal culture or language, and until the cultures fuse, we must keep religion in the language we use. When the economic, educational, etc., experiences have leveled out and equalled up, the cultures *will* fuse. The only reason we have a different culture now is because we have a rotten break, a different experience. Until the experiences level out and justice prevails and people forget color, then there will be no forgetting culture. This culture will be perpetuated as long as the differences are as arbitrarily established and enforced as they are. This is where black language becomes an important part of black preaching, especially to the black masses.

Black preaching also uses a lot of imagination. The whole culture of West Africa is full of stories, engaging stories, some sung, some told. The history of the black pulpit is a history of utterance that has been highly conditioned by the same kind of storytelling tradition. Thus when a black preacher gets up and says, "I saw John sitting on the Isle of Patmos early one Sunday morning," he is putting into details that which implies, "I was an eye-witness. As an eye-witness I give you a living account." Then he gives a living account that people can relate to.

I taught a course once at a Rochester Catholic seminary called

"The Black Bible and the Black Imagination." The whole purpose of the course was to teach Roman Catholic priest candidates how to tell the Bible story so that it would live a little bit. I had an interesting experience when one of the students came back. It reminded me of the time when the disciples came back and told Jesus, "The very devils were subject unto us." They were surprised because even though Jesus had told them how to do it, they didn't expect victories; so their return was with joy and surprise. This young Italian-American fellow came back to class and he said, "Great experience, but I had one problem. I got to telling the story and those people started 'coming out of their pews at me,' and I took *seventeen* minutes. I wasn't supposed to take but ten. It made the mass go seven minutes late. This meant that all of the cars for the next mass were strung up and down the street because they couldn't get into the parking lot. All because I was up there telling that story." I told him that since this was such a dangerous device, he ought to save it for the last mass, when no one else was coming.

This gift of black Bible story telling is the same kind of thing that you get in the Joel Chandler Harris version of Brer Rabbit. Harris only sat down and wrote what he heard black folk saying. He didn't *create* anything. He was a secretary. The kinds of detail, the kinds of humor, the kinds of pointed utterance we associate with the black imagination in the pulpit are very important. People, to date, regardless of color will listen to a black Bible story and never get tired.

At Princeton Seminary I did a three-lecture series on the black Bible. At the end I gave the students the option of calling out a story so that I could "blackenize" it on the spot. They were delighted and, I think, fed. They would have kept me up there all day. They weren't going anywhere. When they asked for Ezekiel's dry bones, I just climaxed on that one and sat down on my own over their protest. This is the sort of thing the whole world needs. The black preacher must not lose his touch at doing it.

The Future of Black Preaching

Just a few words now on the future of black preaching. At this moment black preaching is in the beginning of a major renaissance. That which we are trying to do at our seminary is paralleled in many of the major schools across our nation. Instead of sending men out from the best seminaries to sound "white" and flunk out in the black pulpit, we are sending them out to preach in the "mother tongue" to ordinary folk. In my city, when people heard that seminary students were going to preach, they usually went the other way. Now you can draw a *crowd* by announcing that a seminary student is preaching. We have student preachers who have the best of everything. Some can translate Paul Tillich into biblical blackese and preach it with power. Some can correlate this with the Bible and cause people to learn things they never would have known otherwise. These fellows are quite relevant; they know what black folk need, and how to give it to them. They can be most effective because no one else in the black community can come near the black pulpit in terms of influence and effect. You can be sure that these fellows will be using that influence for any necessary activities related to the kingdom of God.

In addition to the renaissance in curriculum, the seminaries are recruiting young blacks as never before, even Southern Baptist seminaries. At one time my seminary never had more than four black students. Today we have forty. We have more than any non-black seminary in the nation and more than all black seminaries except one. We have six full-time black faculty, but we are still out beating the bushes and recruiting black fellows for ministerial preparation. A great many of these fellows will go out bi-vocationally qualified. Some will have social service degrees, or degrees in law, or business. They will be able to take churches that never really had skilled leadership and lead them to Kingdom greatness while still practicing their second professions.

If this present trend continues, I see in the future of the black church a tremendous growth in the pulpit. It is also true that our accomplishments are getting much better coverage than they once did. A fellow like Jesse Jackson whose whole base of operation is built on his preaching, as little as some people might realize it, is the sort of person who causes many young men to say, "You know if I could do that, I might let the Lord call me."

The preaching ministry is no longer a thing to be done only when you can't pass medical school tests. We will continue to draw more and more seminary students and provide better and relevant training. For this I thank God and look with great joy to the future.

One other thing I would like to suggest is that whatever we do in the seminaries is bound to influence the white student as well as the black. I took part in a workshop this year combining the black and white preaching labs. By far the more eager students who wanted to come in and go over their outlines before they preached them, who sat and listened to every pearl on black preaching, were the white students.

We have quite a mixture at our seminary. There are the high church Episcopal who have Eucharist a couple of days a week. Then we have just regular white Protestant services a couple of times a week. On Wednesday, we have "high holy day." That's the day we "have church." There are more people who come to "church" on Wednesday than any of the other services. I should have pointed this out earlier: while I said that whites have scrupulously avoided looking at blacks as models for anything, on the seminary campus today a great many whites are beginning to recognize the tremendous power of the black church and the black pulpit.

The Episcopalians are really taking this very seriously. Dr. Gardner Taylor had six white Episcopalians in one course last year. He happens to teach at our school in addition to the six full-time black men. With this happening it is quite conceivable that the white Protestant church, which in some instances is really in death throes statistically (because the Jesus Movement in most cases is not related to the church), may yet be brought back to life. The black church may offer the saving possibility to other racial church traditions as well.

5 • Music in the Black Church

JOSEPH C. PYLES

Over one half of black church membership is in various Baptist denominations. Of the many activities in the black community, music is the unifying medium. The black worship experience is poetic and musical throughout. Everything that occurs within black worship either is or becomes poetry and music. The black preacher of yesterday was limited in some ways. His limitations forced him to memorize his sermon, consequently his presentations took on a singsong nature. Whether it was talking, praying, or proclaiming the gospel, utterances eventually turned into singing. The persistence of musical character is a distinctively creative aspect of black worship.

Music in black worship offers a splendid variety. It runs the gamut from classical hymns and anthems to the sophisticatedly arranged spirituals, from the raw, unadulterated spirituals to the black metered hymn; from the jazzy to the improvised gospels. All of these types of music are rendered and appreciated in black churches. There is no other church where such a variety of music is integrated, presented, and sustained within a unified experience of worship. The black churches which I know do not force the worshiper to choose between J. S. Bach and James Cleveland (a famous current black gospel songwriter and artist). The black worshiper is free to move easily among all types of music produced out of the free Protestant spirit of religious expression.

The anthem has a place in the worship of most independent black Methodist and Baptist congregations. The mastery of the anthem represents to the black choir the same kind of achievement as the rendering of "The Earl Koenig" represents to Robert Bradley and Roland Hayes.

To be able to sing anthems indicates a high level of technical, progressive, liberated, and educated musical attainment. The Christmas oratorio and the Easter cantata are annual events which, along with the weekly use of an anthem, represent emancipation, education, and the freedom to understand and reflect the highest in white musical culture. The worshipers who tolerantly listen to the anthems take just as much pride in being able to listen as do the musicians who perform them. Their presence in the worship service is an indication that the congregation has "arrived." Sometimes the communal contemplation of a familiar biblical text of an anthem, plus the pride and joy at having "arrived," intensifies into shouting on the anthem in certain churches known to be spiritually and emotionally uninhibited.

Congregational Singing

The standard Protestant hymn also finds its place in the black worship experience. Such hymns as:

"Holy, Holy, Holy"
"The Church's One Foundation"
"Faith of Our Fathers"
"Rejoice, Ye Pure in Heart"
"A Mighty Fortress Is Our God"
"Lead on, O King Eternal"
"Love Divine, All Loves Excelling"

"O God, Our Help in Ages Past"
"All Hail the Power"
"O Love That Wilt Not Let Me Go"
"I Love Thy Kingdom, Lord"
"Beneath the Cross of Jesus"
"Jesus, I My Cross Have Taken"

These are usually sung by the choirs and congregation as they are written with few or no embellishments. They do not lend themselves to improvisation, and are not readily mutated beyond recognition. In the worship service they represent the versatility of the black worshiper in his ability to move freely between two worlds. An almost exclusive use of these hymns might suggest that the given black congregation has lost its flexibility in an overly anxious attempt to identify wholly with white culture as a sign of emancipation.

One influence for music in the black worship experience is the

white revivalistic hymn learned from the white evangelistic missionary. These hymns are typified by:

"A New Name in Glory"	"One Day"
"Are You Washed in the Blood?"	"My Hope Is Built on Nothing
"Yield Not to Temptation"	Less"
"God Will Take Care of You"	"Nothing but the Blood"
"Blessed Assurance"	"Pass Me Not, O Gentle Saviour"
"Down at the Cross"	"The Old Rugged Cross"
"He Lives"	"Saved, Saved"
"He Lifted Me"	"Since Jesus Came into My Heart"
"Higher Ground"	"When We All Get to Heaven"
"In the Garden"	"The Name of Jesus"
"I Must Tell Jesus"	" 'Tis So Sweet to Trust in Jesus"
"Jesus Is All the World to Me"	"We're Marching to Zion"
"Love Lifted Me"	"What a Friend We Have in Jesus"
"Lead Me to Calvary"	

These songs are musically freer, more emotional, and embrace
a personal theology. They lend themselves easily to many improvisations and mutations. Placed in the spiritual context of an en-
thusiastic black congregation, they may be sung with syncopated or
"stop time" rhythms and may be rendered at a much slower or
faster pace than the composer intended, depending upon the mood
of the congregation. They are not always recognizable after under-
going improvisation.

The early black worshipers moved from the white evangelical or
revivalistic hymn to the black hymn composed by trained black
clergymen and laymen. Many of these hymns have not been published in white hymn books and are therefore unfamiliar to whites.
They are often unknown and disregarded. I have seen no written
study of these and of their value to Protestant religion, but to black
worshipers, they represent a rich musical and theological heritage.
I refer to such hymns as are published in the *Baptist Standard Hymnal*
(published in 1924 by the Sunday School Publishing Board of the
National Baptist Convention, U.S.A.), *The Gospel Pearls* (published
in 1921 by the same publisher), and *The African Methodist Episcopal
Hymnal* (revised and published by the A.M.E. Sunday School Union
in 1954). Some examples of these black hymns are:

"Some Day"
"We'll Understand It Better By and
    By"
"Take Your Burden to the Lord and
    Leave It There"
"Hold to God's Unchanging Hand"
"I Will Trust in the Lord"
"I Feel Like Going On"
"I'll Live On"
"My Loved Ones Are Waiting for
    Me"

"Stand by Me"
"Precious Lord Take My Hand"
"Lift Him Up"
"Is Thy Heart Right with God"
"Never Alone"
"What Are They Doing in Heaven
    Today"
"Think of His Goodness to You"
"Nothing Between"
"I'm Going Through Jesus"
"Life Is Like a Mountain Railroad"

Black hymnology seemed to flourish in the late nineteenth and early twentieth centuries when the above mentioned hymns were written.

A more emotional spirit is experienced as one moves from the black hymn to the black spiritual which represents the bedrock of all black music. For the most part, the black man did not originally have divisions of sacred and secular music. To him, all of his music was sacred. Even when we hear him singing of an experience relating a domestic problem, it is made manifest that he is appealing to a being outside of himself and higher than his slave master. Such as:

> Came home this morning and found the lock changed on my door,
> Came home this morning and found the lock changed on my door.
> My baby left this message, that I don't live there no more.
> Lawd, have mercy; Lawd, have mercy, please.

Miles Mark Fisher, author of *Negro Slave Songs in the United States,* acknowledges that black spirituals have furnished the initial tune vocabulary for all kinds of black songs. It is the "mother music" of all the other forms of black musical creativity. These songs have the following salient characteristics:

1. They originated within the experience of slavery. They are thus "slave songs" and represent music conceived in pain, born of suffering, and characterized by pathos. This music is akin to the music of Israel. The table of contents of the Hebrew songbook (Psalms) could to some great extent be identified with that of the

black man in America.

2. They have biblical and/or theological content. Like the black sermon they are built around biblical themes of: creation, deliverance, miracles (Jacob wrestling with the angel or Joshua at the battle of Jericho), the calling of the prophets, the birth of Christ, baptism, communion, the experience of salvation, the coming of Christ, life in the upper bright world.

Later, some of these original spirituals were mutated into work songs and other secular types, but this does not contradict the contention that they were originally spirituals, and thus religious in character, message, tune, and rhythm.

3. They are anonymous and represent the productivity of the group rather than the musical genius of an individual. This is, however, not an absolute distinction as the groups had to be inspired by a charismatic individual, and the individual had to be emotionally and artistically influenced by the group. They are thus the spontaneous expression of the group and also the work of individual talented composers. The production of spirituals represents a symbiosis of the talented individual leader and the sensitive group. An example of how the leader and the group cooperated in the singing and probably the production of the slave songs can be illustrated:

> *Leader:* Swing low, sweet chariot
> *Group:* Coming for to carry me home.
> *Leader:* Swing low, sweet chariot
> *Group:* Coming for to carry me home.
> *Leader:* I looked over Jordan, what did I see
> *Group:* Coming for to carry me home?
> *Leader:* A band of angels coming after me
> *Group:* Coming for to carry me home.

Most students of the slave songs maintain that they are indeed anonymous. A notable exception to this theory is Miles Mark Fisher's contentions that the internal "evidence" of the spiritual can be correlated with the external history in such a way as to specify the composer, place, time, and situation of the spirituals.

Spirituals speak of life and death, Not only was the black slave looking forward to "a day around God's throne," but Christianity had given him a hope of a brighter day on earth. Could it have been he expressed this hope when he sang this song?

> I've got shoes, you've got shoes,
> All of God's chilluns got shoes
> When we git to heaven, gonna put on my shoes;
> And walk all over God's heaven?

Was it hope springing within the eternal breast that caused him to sing, "We are climbing Jacob's ladder"? Fisher suggests that "Steal Away" was most assuredly written by Nat Turner in 1825 at Southampton County, Virginia, on the occasion of his call to be a prophet. Granted, this is a reconstruction based on pure conjecture. So far as we are able to prove, the spirituals must remain anonymous with no conclusive evidence identifying the composers, dates, places, or circumstances.

4. The spirituals are simplistic. The austere simplicity of the spirituals accounts for their astounding beauty. Musically, they represent the most amazing economy of tonal intervals. The intervals between notes are very short and the variety of tones is indeed scarce. Thus the spirituals are easy to learn, remember, and transmit. This accounts for the fact that while many of them are yet unpublished, they still exist in the historical memory of the black community and are being handed down to the present generation by octogenarians who learned them in their childhood. Some published and familiar spirituals are:

"Deep River"	"Every Time I Feel the Spirit"
"Go Down, Moses"	"Were You There?"
"Joshua Fit de Battle of Jericho"	"O Freedom"
"We Are Climbing Jacob's Ladder"	"O What a Beautiful City"
"Swing Low"	"Down by the Riverside"
"There's No Hiding Place down Here"	"Wade in the Water"
	"Let Us Break Bread Together"
"It's Me, O Lord"	"Nobody Knows the Trouble I See"
"Roll, Jordan, Roll"	"My Lord, What a Morning"
"Steal Away to Jesus"	"Sit Down Servant"

Some unfamiliar and/or unpublished spirituals are:

"Let Jesus Lead You"
"Heaven Belongs to You"
"Pray, Somebody, Pray"
"The Blood's Done Signed My
Name"
"Lord, I Can't Stay Away"
"Press On"
"I'll Meet You There"
"See How They Done My Lord"
"Got to Go to Judgment"
"Oh, Lord"
"Crown Him Lord of All"

"When My Heart Is Burdened
Down"
"Gonna Tell It"
"Mighty Rocky Road"
"Way in the Kingdom"
"In a Time Like This"
"One of These Days"
"Christ the Lord's Done Set Me
Free"
"The Good Old Ship of Zion"
"I'm Going to Stay on the Battle-
field"

Gospel Music

As the worshiper climbs from the black spiritual to highly animated, rhythmically snycopated gospels which are modern jazz improvisations of spirituals and hymns, a new emotional high is experienced. These songs represent religious adaptions of hard rock jazz. Gospels are characterized by the following features:

Folk vocal style rather than concert style
Call and response patterns
Polyrhythms or simultaneous rhythms
Hard and pronounced syncopation
Ostinato figures (repeated musical patterns)
Percussion, hand clapping, shouting, and stamping
Liberal improvisation and variation
Man-centered rather than God-centered ideas (reflecting human
trauma)

Gospel music has been popularized, secularized, and commercialized by such artists as Clara Ward, James Cleveland, Mahalia Jackson, Rosetta Thorpe, and Harold Smith. They have won wide acceptance and acclaim in the white world, and this has accelerated their value in the black church which gave them birth.

Yesterday, the black man was not as free at worship as he is today. He was taught that his style of singing and preaching was barbarous and ignorant. Submitting himself to this criticism he would not express his inner feelings when in the presence of his white contemporaries. Perhaps it seemed on many occasions, he was asked to sing songs of Zion in a strange land. When he refused, a spiritual awakening caused him to realize "not to sing would be to forget Jerusalem," and before he would allow this to happen, he would much rather his tongue lose its ability to articulate and his hands forget their ability to handle the instrument.

The "Hard Rock Gospel Jazz" Conflict

This brings us to a discussion of an unfortunate conflict now going on in the black community between traditional music and the hard rock gospel jazz. There was a time when gospels were not allowed in sophisticated black churches or on black college campuses. If spirituals were sung in either the pretentious church or on the dignified campus, they were so designed and arranged as to have assumed classical European musical form. But as gospels became secularized and commercialized, they acquired status and acceptance in the white world and found their way into "silk stocking" black churches and college campuses.

Recently, gospel choirs have been formed on college and university campuses. These have quickly become the most popular musical ensemble on the campus. They are in great demand from every department of the university, and whenever they are scheduled to sing they draw capacity crowds. They are also called upon to sing frequently in functions off campus. They do not sing tamed gospels with a simple straight-time beat, but the accentuated and polyrhythmic patterns of hard rock, jazzy, unmitigated gospels. One cannot effectively sing gospels in a detached attitude of the cool manipulator of an alien musical or thematic form. One has to enter into the substance and nitty-gritty of the rhythm and the message in order to sing gospels convincingly. It is not uncommon for those who sing them to go into a frenzy. The elements of gospel music are capable of producing a state of ecstasy. Men and women screaming, falling to the floor, running and shouting, are not infrequent.

The emergence of the gospel movement on the college campus

has temporarily put the traditional university choir out of business. This traditional ensemble is not presently functioning as usual due to certain administrative complications. But this conflict which is occurring at some campuses and in some few black churches will be resolved as the younger black, trained in both classicals and gospels, develops a music organizational structure that will accommodate the skilful rendering of both types. The black church has demonstrated the ability to do this again and again.

The conflict on some campuses is really unnecessary and will be of short duration because the students required to sing in the university choir are quite willing to sing in the gospel choir also. The current student, living in the brave new world of the soul movement, has no difficulty singing either J. S. Bach or James Cleveland and can move easily from one to the other. The black church with its musical versatility has prepared and conditioned the black student to such breadth and tolerance. The older authoritarian who fled from the black church because of its lack of sophistication is unable now to move from anthem to gospel because the latter seems to him to repudiate his training and his social goals. He allowed his schooling to alienate him from spontaneous musical forms and liberal improvisations.

However, the new black awareness has produced a new professional black musician who can perform the European classics admirably and just as skillfully produce the spontaniety and unpredictable improvisations of gospel music-making. They have given to gospel music certain embellishments that only a trained musician can afford: authentic harmonizations, clever chord progressions, creative cadenzas.

In like manner they have taken "soul power" into classical musical forms and made them come alive spiritually. This is the genius of Paul Robeson, Marian Anderson, Roland Hayes, Leontyne Price, and many others. These black musicians have infused "soul" into standard white musical forms and have sung them with a certain indescribable "something within" that makes them outstanding. A Simmons University coed, the prima donna for "Inflammatus" was singing in the auditorium of the West Chestnut Street Baptist Church in Louisville, Kentucky. She hit a high "C" and held onto it with vocal skill intensified by "soul power." A black preacher who was previously inhibited by his schooling and culture, arose to his feet, made his way from the rear of the church, came down to the front of the auditorium, raised both hands to heaven, and cried aloud, "It's all right."

This is the greatness of the black musician. If he doesn't let himself get hung-up on choosing between one or the other, he can perform well in a variety of musical mediums. This is what has been going on all the time in the mainline black church which did not train itself away from spontaneity or improvise itself away from training.

6·The Black Church's Outreach

W. J. HODGE

How shall we sing the Lord's song in a strange land? If I forget thee, O Jerusalem, let my right hand forget her cunning. If I do not remember thee, let my tongue cleave to the roof of my mouth; if I prefer not Jerusalem above my chief joy (Ps. 137:4–6).

Now when Ebed–melech the Ethiopian, one of the eunuchs which was in the king's house, heard that they had put Jeremiah in the dungeon; the king then sitting in the gate of Benjamin; Ebed-melech went forth out of the king's house, and spake to the king, saying, My lord the king, these men have done evil in all that they have done to Jeremiah the prophet, whom they have cast into the dungeon; and he is like to die for hunger in the place where he is: for there is no more bread in the city. The king commanded Ebed–melech the Ethiopian, saying, Take from thence thirty men with thee, and take up Jeremiah the prophet out of the dungeon, before he dies. So Ebed–melech took the men with him, and went into the house of the king under the treasury, and took thence old cast clouts and old rotten rags, and let them down by cords into the dungeon to Jeremiah. And Ebed–melech the Ethiopian said unto Jeremiah, Put now these old cast clouts and rotten rags under thine armholes under the cords. And Jeremiah did so. So they drew up Jeremiah with the cords, and took him up out of the dungeon: and Jeremiah remained in the court of the prison (Jer. 38:7–13).

The Spirit of the Lord is upon me, because he has anointed me to preach the gospel to the poor; he hath sent me to heal the broken-hearted, to preach deliverance to the captives, and recovering of sight to the blind, to set at liberty them that are bruised, to preach the acceptable year of the Lord (Luke 4:18–19).

73

74 The Black Christian Experience

One of the strange, weird, perplexing, and paradoxical miracles of history is the origin of the black church on the North American continent. The dehumanizing, brutal, and barbaric fashion in which blacks were captured, bought, shipped, and subsequently treated in the New World would seem to mitigate forever against their acceptance of the religion their masters were supposed to have had. If Cowper's famous "God moves in a mysterious way, His wonders to perform," needed any historical validation, the black church is it.

Anyone who reads a history of the black church will discover that its very origin was akin to the movement of the Christian faith beyond the narrow confines of Judaism in the first century. In that historic conference in Jerusalem as recorded in Acts 15, Simon Peter posed a question which found relevance in the first days of black Baptists and Methodists. Peter asked: "Now therefore why tempt ye God, to put a yoke upon the neck of the disciples, which neither our fathers nor we were able to bear?"

When Andrew Bryan was ordained on January 20, 1788, recognized, and invested with full authority to preach the gospel and to administer the ordinances of the Baptist church, there was a simultaneous fear that Bryan's work would only result in that of "servile insurrection." Slaves were arrested and severely punished for attending the meetings of this black Baptist preacher's church. Carter G. Woodson records that "Andrew Bryan and his brother Sampson, a deacon, were inhumanely cut and their backs were so lacerated that their blood ran down to the earth as they, with uplifted hands, cried to the Lord; but Bryan in the midst of his torture declared that he rejoiced not only to be whipped but would freely suffer death for the cause of Jesus Christ." [1] The courage of Andrew and Sampson Bryan was equal to that of Peter and John as recorded in Acts 4.

The origin of African Methodists is no less heroic. Pulled from their knees as they prayed, Richard Allen, Absalom Jones, and William White led a group of black worshipers out of the Methodist Church, which was to culminate in the organization of the African

Methodist Episcopal Church in 1816.

In 1796, another step of seccession from white-dominated Methodism was taken by black members of the Johns Street Methodist Episcopal Church in New York City. This led to the organization of the African Methodist Episcopal Zion Church.

African Methodism came into being because of an insatiable desire for independence. At first they had white Methodist preachers with local preachers of color serving under them. They notified the white Methodists that they no longer felt themselves obligated to look to them for supplying the pulpit.

It is not my function to do an exhaustive statement on the history of the black church. These three instances of origins, one in the South, two in the North, as well as subsequent origins of associations and conventions, dramatize and authenticate the assertion that the very origin of the black church was a movement of liberation and quasi-black religious nationalism. Negroes were in a strange, weird land, and having no African Jerusalem for which their hearts yearned, they did sing the Lord's song by the waters of the Mississippi.

It has been asserted that the black church has been an opiate for black people, dulling their senses to their miserable plight on earth. Joseph R. Washington, Jr., in his *Black Religion,* says, "Virtually from the beginning Negroes were introduced to the rewards of Christianity for the good of the planters in this world and for the good of the slaves in the world beyond."

Considering the brutality, the dehumanization, the satanic evil of slavery; the debauchery of Reconstruction with the development of a system of politics fashioned on grandfather clauses, poll taxes, and white primaries; inane legal definitions of "Negroes"; the development of a system of education designed to perpetuate the evil myth of racial superiority and inferiority and a degrading isolation from the avenues of entrance into the American system; the development of an economic system based on: the resurrection of the old plantation, ill-gotten gains hatched out of the sharecropper bag, mere survival by menial labor, servitude by being domestics who found pieces of money "lost" by "Miss Jane" to encourage stealing, thus trying them with an iniquitous bond of loyalty—if the black church did no more than help us survive these by promises of a better world beyond, it is no less valid than the vision of John in Revelation during the Neronian and Diocletian persecutions.

The paradox is that though black preaching and worship were so conceived by white America, they stood in fear of the rise of the Negro church. In 1800 Gabriel Prosser, a slave, planned a revolt in Richmond, Virginia, which was betrayed by two slaves. Prosser used the "Bible to describe how slaves could assume the posture of the Israelites and discharge the bonds of slavery with the aid and comfort of God." [2]

In 1822 Denmark Vesey led an uprising in Charleston, South Carolina. According to Washington, members of the Negro Methodist Church were involved.

We are all familiar with Nat Turner, who led a bloody revolt at Southampton County, Virginia in 1831. Nat Turner was a Baptist exhorter and a mystic. It is said that he spent months in prayer and Bible reading before he even planned the insurrection.

Any good history book on the South will validate the assertion about fear. In 1833, Alabama made it unlawful for slaves or free Negroes to preach unless before respectable slaveholders and when authorized by some neighboring religious society. In 1834, Georgia enacted a law providing that neither free Negroes nor slaves might preach or exhort an assembly of more than seven unless licensed by justices on the certification of three ordained ministers. Other Southern states soon followed these examples, passing more drastic laws prohibiting the assembly of Negroes after the early hours of the night, and providing for the expulsion of all free Negroes from such commonwealths, so as to reduce the danger of mischief and the spread of information by this more enlightened class. In *From Slavery to Freedom,* John Hope Franklin says that between 1830 and 1835 most states had outlawed Negro preachers.

My contention to this point is that the black church's outreach has always extended beyond the bounds of correct doctrine, Bible teaching, and Sunday meetings. When you talk about the black man's God, in his most authentic expression, he has always been a God of liberation, to set the captives free.

Equally as miraculous as its origin, has been the outreach of the black church. Among many other sources, one has only to read Frazier's *The Negro Church in America*, to see the obstacles which had to be overcome.

1. There was, first of all, the damage done in the selling, buying, and transporting of slaves from Africa. They were bought for beads and rum. According to Frazier "they were held in baracoons, a euphemistic term for concentration camps at the time, where slaves, without any regards for sex, or family and tribal affiliation were kept until some slaver came along to buy a cargo for the markets of the New World. This period of dehumanization was followed by the 'middle passage,' the voyage across the Atlantic Ocean to the slave markets of the West Indies and finally the indigo, tobacco, and cotton plantations of what was to become the United States of America. During the 'middle passage,' Negroes were packed spoon-fashion in the slave ships where no regard was shown for sex or age differences. . . ." [3]

2. The second barrier to the development of "peoplehood" was the size of the plantation and their orientation into their new university of Christian slavery. The majority of slaves were on small farms and small plantations. Thus, contact was minimized.

It is reported that new slaves were gradually accustomed to work. They were made to bathe often, to take long walks, and especially to dance. They were distributed in small numbers among old slaves in order to dispose them better to acquire their habits.

3. They were prohibited from preserving or using their own language. This was done in order to better tap their lines of communication.

4. The plantation system was specifically designed to loosen all social bonds among them and to destroy their traditional basis of social cohesion.

5. The mobility of the slave system was highly prohibitive of any

cohesion as well as a concept of a black slave by a white owner. Bancroft, in his *Slave Trading in the Old South,* quotes from *The Charleston Mercury,* which states, ". . . slaves are as much and as frequently articles of commerce as the sugar and molasses which they produce." [4]

6. The American slave system made insecure and precarious the most elementary form of social life, the family. There was no legal marriage. All relationships were temporary, dependent upon the will of the white masters and the exigencies of the plantation regime.

Sheares and others, in the November 2–16, 1970 issue of *Christianity and Crisis,* point out additional barriers imposed by the white church itself:

1. The exclusion of blacks from the ethical and moral protection of the church.

2. Provision of divine sanction and reinforcement for the system of slavery.

3. The incorporation into its own life and practices the separatist ways of society, the establishment of "nigger balconies," and the denial of "equal accommodations" and equal access to the ministerial services and resources of the church. "Negro pews" were often painted black, a derogatory sign in those days. Frequently blacks were not allowed to enter the church at all; they listened through open doors and windows. Whites refused to share the Lord's Supper with them. Slaves took the Lord's Supper in the church basement or after the whites had gone home.

Despite these and other restrictions, such as fugitive slave laws, laws of illegal assembly, the lack of formal education, little or no money, repression of expression, the preachments of an illegitimate theology, the black church developed and stretched forth its wings. The outlawing of black preachers and assembly without the presence of five whites, was a tacit admission of the recognition of the explosive, revolutionary power of the gospel of Jesus Christ by the white power structure of that day. Somehow, by God's grace working through the black slaves and some white liberated Christians, the slaves discovered the explosive power of this gospel and stretched forth their wings of obedience to the Great Commission.

Educational Outreach

These so called unlearned, unlettered, nonhuman beings, developed schools to teach themselves and their offsprings. George Lyle, a black Baptist preacher, organized and taught in a free school. Dr. Henry Adams, the first pastor of Fifth Street Baptist Church, Louisville, Kentucky, organized the first school for Negroes in that city.

African Methodism founded such schools as: Wilberforce in Ohio, 1856; Allen University in South Carolina, 1881; Morris Brown, Atlanta, Georgia, 1885; Livingston College, North Carolina, 1889; and Lane College, Tennessee, 1889.

Negro Baptists founded and organized such schools as: Selma University, Alabama, 1879; Arkansas Baptist College, Arkansas, 1884; State University, Louisville, Kentucky, 1873; Guadalupe College, Sequin, Texas, 1885; Virginia Theological Seminary, Lynchburg, Virginia 1891; Friendship College, Rock Hill, South Carolina, 1891; Woman's National Training School, Washington, D.C., 1909; and Morris College, South Carolina.

There were other schools, of course, founded and operated for Negro Baptists by the American Baptist Home Mission Society. Such schools as Benedict College, South Carolina; Bishop College, now in Dallas; Shaw University, Spellman Seminary (for girls); Virginia Union University; Roger Williams University, burned in 1905, and reorganized under the control of Negro Baptists in Tennessee.

In 1947 the late Carter G. Woodson, black historian par excellence, had this to say of the Negro church:

> The Negro Church, handicapped as it has been, has accomplished some things impossible. In spite of the increasing influence of the public schools with largely augmented resources the church schools have continued and in poverty have produced the outstanding men of the race. (This is reminiscent of the Master's message to the church of Smyrna in Revelation—'I know thy works, and tribulation, and poverty—but thou art rich.') With their limited resources these

church schools report a large number of influential ministers than those richly endowed." [5]

Outreach in Significant Generalities

In 1945, Carter Woodson made the bold claim that "most movements among Negroes owe their success to the leadership of Negroes prominent in the Church." W. R. Pettiford, a preacher in Alabama, became one of the pioneer Negro bankers. This was true of the late Dr. Henry Boyd and many others.

The black church has served as a newspaper, a forum for black expression, a school for the development of orators, who have impressed the world as the inspired spokesmen of a persecuted people. For many decades it was the only welfare agency we had. Even now, in crises situations, it serves this purpose.

Wherever you find a black owned and operated hospital, the church was a source of inspiration, funds, and public relations. Rural, small towns, and big city churches formed burial and benevolent societies, credit unions, and insurance companies.

From my own small town, rural background, I know that the church gave support to young physicians, morticians, teachers, and small businessmen.

In earlier years, many blacks regularly attended church whether Christian or sinners. Barred from other social centers, they went to church to see their friends. Having no automobiles, or parks, or theaters, a young man went to church to meet his sweetheart, to impress her with his worth, and woo her in marriage. The church was the school of agriculture for many farmers who had to depend upon the black farm agent for new information on growing crops or the reception of new government regulations. There was a time when, almost literally, the church was his "all and all."

The Black Church and the Freedom Movement

I go back to the freedom—civil rights—liberation movement because of the recent avalanche of criticism about the irrelevancy and impotence of the black church. If I were to say that the black church has lived up to its calling, I would be reckless with the truth. Nobody is more painfully aware of the shortcomings of the black church than the black preacher. But to say that it never has been and is not now a significant part of this movement is to ignore the truth.

The black church has always been possessed by a significant degree of radicalism and militancy. In 1830, on September 15, Negro delegates met in the Bethel Church in Philadelphia to launch a series of conventions aimed at freedom. They advised some brothers to go to Canada. They condemned the American Colonization Society. They deprecated segregation as unjust, oppressive, and unconstitutional. They stressed the importance of education, temperance, and economy. Believe it or not, they set aside the Fourth of July as a day of "humiliation, fasting, and prayer," when Negroes would ask for divine intervention to break the shackles of slavery.

We are familiar with the rise of Dr. Martin L. King, Jr., and the Southern Christian Leadership Conference. Now as then, its leadership, base, and backbone was the black church. Martin Luther King talked about the power of nonviolence as Gandhi taught it, but when people marched, protested, demonstrated, and held their freedom rallies, it was always to the words and rhythm of the Negro spiritual.

One of the most creative aspects of SCLC is "Breadbasket." It is basically church oriented and led by leaders of tremendous resourcefulness such as Jesse Jackson in Chicago, Bill Jones in New York, Andrew Brown in Indianapolis, and many whose names we have not heard.

The heroic struggle in Cairo, Illinois, is led by a black preacher.

One of the most powerful movements among us has been that of the Pullman car porters led by that venerable statesman, A. Phillip Randolph. For many years they had no place to meet but the black church and a few lodge halls. I think they would testify to the power of the church's extended arm.

At this moment, black churches in Los Angeles, Detroit, Kansas City, Atlanta, Pittsburgh, Dallas, Cincinnati, Louisville, and in other cities have built and are building low-cost, subsidized rental apartments, nursing homes, and apartments for the elderly. My own church, Fifth Street Baptist in Louisville, initiated and co-sponsors a high-rise apartment, known as the Blanton House, for the elderly. It will be twenty stories high and the cost exceeds $3,000,000.

My own involvement in the freedom-liberation movement since 1946 has been mostly with NAACP. I made a check of the officers of our branches and found that almost one third of them were black preachers. Churches across the land have taken out life memberships in the NAACP. The NAACP would have been but a ripple in the mighty waters of justice if it had not been for the black church. The chairman of our board is Bishop Spottswood of the African Methodist Episcopal Zion Church. Gloster Current, director of our branches, is an ordained clergyman. Clarence Mitchell, called the 101st U.S. Senator and who carries more weight in our nation's capitol than the Black Congressional Caucus, is an active churchman and dedicated Christian. And anybody who listens to Roy Wilkins, our executive director, these days and watches him in action, knows that he is possessed of Christ.

What more should I say? . . . the black church extending the kingdom of God in its native land through the preaching of the gospel and its worship; the black church establishing its own publishing boards and printing its own literature; the black church, victimized because of the color and background of servitude of its members, sending missionaries to its Motherland, India, Haiti, the Bahama Islands, South America; the black church rearing up new prophets who are scholars like Cone, Washington, Wright, Mitchell, Roberts, Johnston, Thurman, Scott, Long, Eichelberger, Proctor, Walker, Mays, Kelsey, McClain, Watts, who are evangelicals of a more relevant theology and promoters with a passion!

I do not mean to glamorize or put a halo where one should not be. My desire is to do my small share of demythologizing the image of the black church given to many of us in white seminaries, popularized by a few black educators and sociologists who knew not the black Joseph, rhetoricalized by a few black militants created by the white press and who, until this day, have not done their homework in black history. It appears they never read Carter Woodson and only certain portions of DuBois. If so, they would have known that the church against which their angry voices have been raised has always sought to change the imposed image of the black man of himself as a thing, to a person of infinite worth because he was made in the image of God who liberates and reconciles men unto himself through Jesus Christ.

The historic function of this church is still a relevant function. Seeing the reverses facing us as symbolized by The Man in Washington and the Man in Montgomery, Alabama, black people must still be inspired to endure, to hold on, to wake up and face the demands of the rising sun. Still faced with backlashes, polarization, and alienation, the black church is called anew as an agent of liberation, however hard or difficult it may be and however much our past oppression and humiliation causes us to rebel.

You may have difficulty understanding the cause of our rebellion at the call to be an apostle of reconciliation. I don't. When I remember my father, a grown man, calling the *children* of the white folks for whom he worked, who were my age, Mr. Joe and Mr. Jack; when I remember having always to go to their back door because we just didn't go to Mr. Charlie's front door; when I remember being sent to the kitchen (where the food was cooked and the dishes were washed) every time I ate at a white restaurant; when I remember a member of our draft board responding to my application for military deferment because I was a ministerial student by presenting it thus to the Chairman of that Board; "Barfield, Barfield, here is a boy, a black boy who wants to be deferred"; when I remember seeing the principal of my high school drive up to a Ford agency and the owner of that agency coming out and seeing him in that brand new Ford saying, "Here comes Nelson. Nelson is a good nigger"; when I remember two Negro prostitutes being run out of town because they were caught with a prominent white lawyer who remained and maintained his prominence; when I remember Negroes receiving five years in the penitentiary for stealing a sack of flour and a white man given two years suspended sentence for killing a Negro; when I remember the white "icehouse" man refusing to put a fifty pound piece of ice in my pick-up truck as he did for the whites and telling me, "Come and get it yourself, nigger-boy"; when I remember streets being paved to the end of the white community and left unpaved in the total Negro community; when I remember seeing a postman, always white, delivering mail only in the white community; it's hard for me to be an apostle of reconciliation, but this is a commandment of our Christ and ambassadors of reconciliation we must be.

We must be the Isaiah comforting the afflicted and the Amos storming the power centers of the ungodly temples of Bethel.

Like Ebed–melech we must pull together from the dungeons of hate and despair—dug by insecure princes and kings.

Unlike Israel of old, we must sing the Lord's song in a strange and hostile land.

Without becoming victims of messianic and convenant people complexes, we must, as did Simon of old, bear the cross of him who died to set men free. For this is the acceptable year of the Lord, the year, the hour, the moment to preach a full-orbed gospel to the poor, the gospel to heal the brokenhearted, a gospel to deliver the captives, give sight to the blind, and set free those who are oppressed.

7·Black Theology

JOHN W. FLEMING

The term "black theology" poses some difficulty, not so much with the adjective "black" as with the noun "theology." The problem is the singular form, implying oneness, sameness. But this is not the case. Black theology, as any other, runs the spectrum from fundamentalism at one end to humanism at the other, with all the varying degrees of differences in between—conservatism, orthodoxy, neoorthodoxy, liberalism.

In the midst of this diversity there is an underlying unity that is peculiar and distinct. The underlying unity is based on the black experience, characterized by some African traits which lingered on in spite of the devastating effects of slavery. This unity is also characterized by the experience evolving from a color-caste system in the South and an ethnic-grouping system in the North, both systems for the black man being summed up in one word: *oppression.*

As a result of this oppression three outlooks have characterized the religious mood of black people: (1) a religion of resignation— which has given up on the good life in this world and placed all of its hope on a life beyond; (2) a religion of accommodation—which attempts to adjust to and appease the status quo, and (3) a religion of liberation—which seeks to break the shackles of oppression.

These three outlooks have always existed side by side in the black community, and still do. But dominance has shifted from time to time. At the present time the third outlook seems to be the dominant trend. At least it is the one supported by the most articulate spokesman of black religion, and is the mood which seems to be developing a form of systematic theology. For that reason, I am focusing here on what James Cone has labeled "the theology of liberation." My plan is to select what I consider the essence of this theology as it appears in the works of representative thinkers and then draw the strands together in a concluding statement.

Joseph Washington, Jr., and Theology

Much of the present emphasis on black theology can be traced in a negative sort of way to a book by Joseph Washington, Jr., published in 1964, bearing the title, *Black Religion: The Negro and Christianity in America.* Washington reached three conclusions in that work which have bearing on our thinking: (1) Black religion is a "folk" religion. Its uniqueness is found in its quest for the "elusive but ultimate goal of freedom by means of protest and action." In a word, black religion is ethics-oriented, stressing social protest and socialization. (2) Black religion has no theology. (3) In order to have a theological base the black church needs to merge with the white church.

After the publication of his controversial book, Mr. Washington found himself in a predicament similar to a pedestrian walking down the middle of a busy freeway. He was hit from all sides.

His contribution was the recovery of the ethical emphasis of black religion, an emphasis which had been misunderstood, misinterpreted, and sometimes ignored. Many scholars, including some blacks—particularly Benjamin Mays, had seen black religion as compensatory and accommodating, by-passing this life to concentrate on the hereafter. A few scholarly voices had protested against this wholly other-worldly interpretation of black religion. In his book published in 1953, *Negro Slave Songs in the United States,* Miles Mark Fisher had seen the spirituals as history and as containing hidden messages. The other-worldly language of these songs, he contended, has a this-worldly meaning. For example, from internal evidence, he concluded that "Steal Away" was composed by Nat Turner as a means of calling his followers together. Turner, a mystic, saw "green trees a-bending" as a sign for him to lead the slaves out of bondage, and "poor sinner stands a-trembling" if he refused to obey the divine command. But he knew if the plan failed that the line of the spiritual would become a reality, "I hain't got long to stay here."

Someone else declared that when the slave sang, "You can have the world but give me Jesus," he was not talking about that personality who walked the hills of Palestine in the first century but was yearning for the slave ship which bore the name "Jesus" to carry him back to his homeland.

Just as the two books of the Bible, Daniel and Revelation, contained coded messages for the people to whom they were addressed, the spirituals contained coded messages for the slaves. Henrietta Buckmaster, in support of this thesis, said: "Every Negro church in the slave South learned to speak a disguised language about the 'sweet chariot' that was going to carry me home." [1] But very few scholars prior to Washington could see this unique strand of protest in black religion.

The second conclusion, that black religion has no theology, seemed to have been a serious blunder. Freedom and justice cannot be equated with religion, not even a folk religion. As one voice of opposition so succinctly stated it, "At the heart of black religion is what is at the heart of every religion, a faith capable of giving meaning to the mysteries of life." [2] And that is theology—an intellectual unfolding through faith to the point where one comes into some understanding of life's mysteries. Though crudely expressed at times, black religion had this faith. Even the black man's everyday language is sprinkled with such theological terms: God, redemption, regeneration, sin.

His third conclusion, assimilation of the black church with the white church as the solution to his "no theology" criticism, would be funny if it were not so pathetic. As Mr. Washington has discovered since, the white church has no monopoly on Christian theology. Robert N. Bellah, writing in *Daedalus*,[3] emphasized the fact that the white community also has a civil religion which has developed a theology of its own and which operates both in and outside of the white church. Furthermore, the American religious scene has never been noted for having a heavy theological flavor. H. Richard Niebuhr reminded us some years ago: "The church, as an organization interested in self-preservation and in the gain of power, has sometimes found the counsel of the cross quite as inexpedient as have national and economic groups." [4]

We, then, must disagree with Washington's conclusion that "it is incumbent upon the Negro now to close his house of worship and enter the white congregation of his choice en masse." [5]

Washington's second book, *The Politics of God,* hinted at a change in his thinking. He saw a conflict in the historic religion of the black man and the Western tradition of reason found both in humanism and Protestantism. Implying that since these differences may take a long time to resolve, Washington announced that he was turning his attention to the development of a theology relevant to the needs of the black church and to the subcommunity of Afro-America. He claimed that his second book was not a retraction of the first but ". . . a candid recognition that black religion via separate institutions will be with us for some time." [6]

Continuing in an apologetic vein, Washington went on to add: "This is not a time for rejoicing in the fact of continuation; it is a time for new responses by black religion to a new situation." [7]

Thus, in line with the title of his book, Washington conceived as his task systematizing a theology of human life and thought about God which will help man to see what God would have him do in the "political" arena to become more fully man.

> The heart of *The Politics of God* is a call to action in the spirit of the genius of the black religion. It is to meet the needs of black people via institutional religious relevance. Religion as central to the black community in the past may be vital in the present to the extent it is relevant to the problems of power and politics.[8]

Never forgetting that black religion in the past was community-centered, Washington sees it as becoming once again the actual catalyst for making black lives more authentic. Thus, he writes:

> Central to *The Politics of God* is a call for a serious theology for black religion. . . . The religion of black people is challenged to rise to new

heights of commitment in overcoming injustice, inequality, and lack of freedom among blacks. Meanwhile, black religion, which has been at the center of the black community, now needs to be a central force for giving black power new life and light in this world.[9]

Washington warns the black community to be on the guard against succumbing to a white materialistic religion which he views as avoidance of the Christian mission of suffering and calls for a "chosen people" concept among blacks built on Isaiah's pattern of the suffering servant. "God has called the Negro as the 'suffering servant,' whereby humankind the world over will consciously, not accidentally, voluntarily, not by force as in times past, affirm first in principle and then in practice a life full of human oneness through the biblical way of real knowing." [10]

Black people did not choose this role. God chose black people to be suffering servants. It is through a black-identity affirmation with the suffering role that a cohesiveness will come to the black community. In a word, a meaningful separation on the part of black people can pave the way for a later meaningful integration into the beloved commonwealth by both black and white through the redemptive suffering of blacks.

A prolific writer, Washington has produced a third book on the subject, *Black and White Power Subreption,* in which he continues his effort to systematize a black theology on a Black Power base. Central in his advocacy of such a theology is the cross. As he states it: "In the Cross freedom and power are available as the grace to counter all that keeps us from responding to the source of all freedom, power and truth in its light." [11]

Black Power, as the cross, understands the mission and meaning of suffering. It stands, as did the cross, as evidence that suffering is not a vicarious experience but the result of violence, and that only through violence does suffering come to full meaning and fruition in redemption.[12]

Another aspect of the cross as seen in the Black Power concept ". . . is the dream of a new world and new order born of the old world and old order where men are not divided by the accidents of history but by the accidents of history are brought into a unity of enrichment through diversity." [13]

How far afield Mr. Washington has strayed from the assimilation thesis of his first book! The "unity in diversity" theme of his third book echoes the happy pluralism of Isaiah 11:6—wolves and lambs, leopards and kids, lions and calves living together in harmony.

James H. Cone and Theology

James H. Cone, a black professor at the Union Theological Seminary, New York City, has contributed two volumes to the black theology of liberation: *Black Theology and Black Power* and *Liberation. . . .* He sees as the task of black theology: ". . . to analyze the black man's condition in the light of God's revelation in Jesus Christ with the purpose of creating a new understanding of black dignity among black people, and providing the necessary soul in that people, to destroy white racism." [14]

Cone does not, as Washington did in his first book, draw a rigid line of demarcation between theology and freedom but sees theology as a way of preparing black minds for total commitment to the goal of freedom.

Though more crudely put, Gabriel Prosser, Denmark Vesey, and Nat Turner, black exhorters and leaders of slave rebellions, saw the same relationship between theology and freedom.

Cone argues: "In a society where people are oppressed because they are black, Christian theology must become black theology." [15] In the light of that argument, he defines Christian theology as a theology of liberation. "It is a rational study of the being of God in the world in the light of the existential situation of an oppressed community, relating the forces of liberation to the essence of the gospel, which is Jesus Christ." [16]

With that definition as his base he moves into a discussion of the traditional theological doctrines of God, Jesus Christ, man, the church, the world, and eschatology. The uniqueness of his approach lies in the fact that he sees these doctrines as having no meaning for black people apart from the black experience. As he puts it:

"Black theology is not prepared to discuss the doctrine of God, man, Christ, Church, Holy Spirit—the whole spectrum of Christian theology—without making each doctrine an analysis of the emancipation of black people." [17]

Before that decisive statement, he noted: "Black theology knows no authority more binding than the experience of oppression itself. This alone must be the ultimate authority in religious matters." [18]

The uniqueness of Cone's approach is clearly seen in the discussion of the science of last things. For him, traditional eschatology, with its emphasis on reward and other-worldliness, is irrelevant. He contends that from the black perspective "eschatology comes to mean joining the world and making it what it ought to be. It means that the Christian man looks to the future not for a reward or possible punishment of evil doers, but as a means of making him dissatisfied with the present." [19]

Cone also argues for a new value system, contending that white racism forces black theology in that direction. It would be a value system centered in black self-determination. Black theology within the context of Black Power would be only a temporary measure, for Black Power is a transitional movement. In the terminology of Paul Tillich, Cone calls it a movement from nonbeing to being. Thus, liberation is the key to a black theology of relevance.

Joseph A. Johnson, Jr., and Theology

Dr. Joseph A. Johnson, Jr., a bishop in the CME Church, delivered the Convocation Address at the Andover-Newton Theological School in the autumn of 1969. He added some further insights on the emerging black theology of liberation. As a point of departure, he quoted from a statement on the subject formulated by the National Committee of Black Churchmen.

> For us, Black theology is the theology of liberation. It seeks to plumb the black condition in the light of God's revelation in Jesus Christ, so that the black community can see the gospel is commensurate with the achievement of black humanity. Black theology is a theology of "blackness." It is the affirmation of Black humanity that emancipates

black people from white racism, thus providing authentic freedom for both black and white people in that it says "No" to the encroachment of white oppression.[20]

Here again the uniqueness lies in relating the biblical faith to the black experience. In fact, Johnson said that many white theologians "have felt that this black Christian experience was devoid of meaning and therefore could be omitted in their exposition and interpretation of the Christian faith."[21] But Johnson was emphatic in stating that black theology is a product of black christian experience and reflection. He let his hearers know that it is "no-fly-by-night" development. "It comes out of the past. It is strong in the present and we believe that it is redemptive for the future."[22]

Dr. Johnson's address seemed to classify him as an advocate of a theology which evolves from the existential situation. In fact, he called for a detheologizing of Jesus and a recovery of his humanity. He saw as a starting point Luke 4:18:

> The spirit of the Lord is upon me because he has anointed me; he has sent me to announce good news to the poor,
> to proclaim release for prisoners and recovery of sight for the blind;
> to let the broken victims go free,
> to proclaim the year of the Lord's favour (*The New English Bible*).

This, declared Johnson, was Jesus' universal manifesto of liberation, and liberation expressed the central thrust of his ministry.

It is difficult to call Johnson's statement a formulation of a black theology. It was a sort of existential approach where one finds ground for identifying with the spirit of liberation as evidenced in the life and teachings of Jesus. As Johnson stated it, "to be Christian we must be contemporaneous with Jesus the liberator."[23]

Vincent Harding and Theology

A fourth member of the "new breed" school of black theologians is Vincent Harding, director of the Institute of the Black World, Atlanta, Georgia. Harding has attached a great deal of importance to the communal emphasis of Black Power, the brother and sister relationship of love for each other within the black community. He sees it as a way of abolishing the self-hate and self-shame created by oppression. He does raise an important question about this love.

> If it is assumed—as it surely must be—that black love must begin among black people and find its nurture there, can it be quarantined? What shall be said of a love that is willed towards some people and not towards others? Is this goal in any way related to the deadly disease that has afflicted so much of American life for so many generations? [24]

Harding admits that answers to this dilemma do not come easy but suggests two possible trends: (1) Perhaps a refusal to hate may be a starting point. Under present conditions, refraining from hating may be as much as can be expected of black people. (2) Maybe it is essential to men to have the freedom to hate their enemies before love can become an authentic response. Harding is saying that one must know the negative to really experience the positive.

The theology which evolves from Harding's statement concentrates on man and community. Black Power's religious implication is in producing a new man. But this new man has no meaning apart from community; so the logical extension of the new man is a new community.

With a great deal of honesty he admits that such a community falls short of the ideals of the universal community. But with him, as with the others, Black Power is an interim movement. He reasons that self-hatred among black people has had its extension, hatred for the black community. Then a community of love, even though limited in scope, represents a real step forward.

Harding, with an optimistic outlook, sees in the quest for communal identity of Afro-Americans the "possibility for the coming of a truly religious community," [25] and the seed for a universalism "that is at least as broad as that known by most Western religious traditions." [26]

A provocative question is raised by Harding: "Is it possible that a universalism based on suffering, struggle and hope is more vital than some vague identification based on common links with a possibly dead Creator-Father?" [27]

There is, he contends, a qualified universalism in the Black Power "vivid suggestions of messianism at many points." [28] He refers to Marcus Garvey, a precursor of Black Power, as one who definitely viewed himself as a black messiah. The same strand could be found in Malcolm X, and, though Martin Luther King, Jr., did not view his role as messianic, it was viewed as such by many members of the black community.

Furthermore, there is a sense of expectation in the black community, whether connected with a personal messiah or not, that gives it a messianic tone. Although Harding may not have been aware of it, there is a developing black humanism which sees every black man as a messiah. One spokesman for this school of thought has said:

> Black Humanism . . . does not depend on God and gods to justify its position. It evolves around people and its collective experience rather than "a person," no matter how relevant he may be. We are the Messiah and only we can liberate ourselves. The experiences and insights of all historic figures are useful data for Black Humanism but no single person is the "black savior," neither Jesus nor Buddha nor King nor Malcolm nor anyone but ourselves. [29]

Even though this view falls in the category of way-out as far as the present-day trend in black theology is concerned, it does serve as some indication of the mood of expectancy in, and the messianic tone of, the black community.

With the doctrine of Black Power bent on leading the black community from what is to what ought to be, from an old order to a new order, and with its implied messianic hope, it was natural for Harding to turn his attention to another theological tenet, the doctrine of resurrection. It should not be too difficult for us to see him emphasizing a black resurrection with all of the accompanying glory and power. "And," he writes, "if one follows this invaluable line of thought, it is obvious that Black Power has within it the possibility of setting black men in an entirely new light—the light of their Creator." [30]

As a clinching argument for his religion of Black Power, Harding quotes Dr. Nathan Wright, a noted Episcopal clergyman, scholar, author and the first chairman of the National Conference on Black Power:

> In religious terms, a God of power, of majesty, and of might, who made men to be in His own image and likeness, must will that his creation reflect in the immediacies of life His power, His majesty and His might. Black Power raises . . . the far too long overlooked need for power, if life is to become what in the mind of its Creator it is destined to be.[31]

Albert Cleage, Jr., and Theology

We have saved probably the most controversial of the "new breed" black theologians for the last; Albert Cleage, Jr., pastor of the Shrine of the Black Madonna, Detroit, Michigan.

One who is familiar with Cleage's book, *The Black Messiah,* knows that he stresses the historical Jesus and sees him primarily as one seeking to give the people of Israel power to rebuild the nation. He rejects what he considers to be the Pauline emphasis: "individual salvation and life after death." [32]

> We as black Christians suffering oppression in a white man's land do not need the individualistic and otherworldly doctrine of Paul and the white man. We need to recapture the faith in our power as a *people* and the concept of nation, which are the foundation of the Old Testament and the prophets, and upon which Jesus built all of his teachings 2,000 years ago.[33]

The Old Testament concept of peoplehood and nationhood is not only the central theme of Cleage's work, it is a recurring theme; hence he seeks to establish a black nationalist theology with Jesus in the role of the paradigmatic black revolutionary leader.

In Cleage's thinking, God is a God who acts in history. In answer to the question, "How could the Israelites, a handful of people, still believe that somehow they would emerge triumphant?" he answers: "In every adversity they believed that God was concerned about them. They believed it. They believed that their strength was a strength that their enemies could neither conquer nor destroy because it came from their unique relationship with God." [34]

Because Cleage views Jesus as a black leader of a chosen black nation, black people today are the inheritors of the chosen people legacy.

Cleage pulls no punches in dealing with the question raised by Harding, "Can black love be quarantined?" He argues that it can; indeed, it must:

> I tell you, you cannot love everybody. You have been trying and you feel guilty because you have failed. Forget the guilt feeling. Nobody can love everybody. . . . So why are you sitting around talking about how you have to love everybody? . . .You can't love your enemy. That is ridiculous. Love is only something for inside the nation. We'll try to love each other as much as we can. . . .Outside the nation we are not thinking about love. We are thinking about justice.[35]

Love, then, is the word for interpersonal relationships within the nation. In interpersonal relationships beyond the nation justice is the word.

The matter of identity is also a part of Cleage's theology: "Basic to our struggle and the revitalization of the Black church is the simple fact that we are building a totally new self-image. Our rediscovery of the Black Messiah is a part of our rediscovery of ourselves." [36]

Since this theology lacks an individual stress, Cleage's doctrine of resurrection is the resurrection of a nation, and that in the here and now.

Summary

What can we say in drawing the strands together? We are well aware that theological trends as expressed in the thought of the new breed black theologians are open to criticism. But is this not true of all theological trends? My aim is not criticism but to point to the direction in which black theology is moving.

As I see it, with the possible exception of Harding, all of these thinkers attempt to operate within the framework of traditional

Christianity and to draw heavily on the biblical faith in developing their theology. What they attempt to do is to reinterpret the biblical faith in terms of the black experience, while at the same time, rejecting what appears to be a white nationalist theology that makes allowance for racism. On the other hand, there are other trends which could make up another discussion: for example, the movement stemming from the Black Caucus of the Universal-Unitarian Church, which seemingly is attempting to create a new meaning system apart from the biblical faith; or the religious emphasis from some revolutionaries such as Ron Karenga who view both the black and white church as being beyond redemption and are seeking to create new religious forms which they believe will articulate the spirit of liberation.

But back to the group discussed here—the emerging theology is placing greater stress on the immanence of God, a God who is confronted in life situations. This is not a denial of God's transcendence but a way of saying that his transcendence has been over-stressed at the expense of his immanence. Black theology wants a greater recognition of God who acts in history, who meets us in the suffering and problems of mankind, and with whom we come into an understanding through involvement in humanity.

It is a theology which gives a larger role to man, calling for self-help, self-determination, self-pride. Man is somebody and the aim is to give to the black man or, as with Cleage, to the black nation a sense of belonging. Black theology's theme is liberation, not resignation, not accommodation. Man, the *black* man if you please, must be a participant in the move from nonbeing to being.

With more significance attached to man and his role, there is naturally a strong "this-worldly" emphasis in contemporary black theology. It is a not a negation of eschatology or immortality, but a way of saying, "Seek the good life in the here and now."

Black Power is a central theme in the theology which I have discussed. In fact, Harding equates his theology with Black Power while the others see this concept as meaningful to their theological outlook. It would seem that they view Black Power as the voice within speaking to the needs of the Afro-Americans. Here one also finds the elementary recognition that love without power is sheer sentimentalism just as much as power without love is pure ruthlessness. Black theology contends that the black community and the white community have been victimized by an imbalance of love on the one hand and of power on the other.

Contemporary black theology which stems from the religion of liberation sees God as love and power. It goes further to point out that man created in the godly image must reflect his power as well as his love. Anything less is dehumanizing. A happy balance would mean something like some loving power for black people and some powerful love for white people. There is nothing unilateral about the religious aspects of Black Power. It has some saving grace for the black man, to save him from a love of sentimentalism. It has some saving grace for the white man, to save him from a power of ruthlessness.

Jesus is still portrayed as the ideal but more and more the traditional image of him as lamb, shepherd, and so forth is waning and he is being seen more and more as the liberator.

As indicated earlier, black theology has retained the messianic note so important in Christian thought but the apocalyptic is minimized. The new black theology does not look forward to some cataclysmic, miraculous, and supernatural act through which the old order will be swept out and a new order will be ushered in.

At least two of the thinkers, Washington and Cleage, develop a "chosen people" concept, but they are talking about different things. Washington attempts to relate this concept to the biblical faith of redemptive suffering. He gives practically no clue as to the role of Jesus Christ as the model for the suffering servant and no role of suffering to the church per se. Cleage, supporting his black nationalist theology, traces the genealogy of black people to a black messiah; hence "choseness" is a legacy of inheritance and not a model of suffering. Of course Cleage achieves his objective by placing his own interpretation on biblical history, an interpretation which he does not document. But this man is no fool. He understands the black experience as well as anyone. This understanding has given him some deep insights on the frustrations, hopes, aspirations and needs of black people in the inner city. His chosen people idea appeals to the black awareness mood of the inner city.

While there is a social emphasis in all these theologians, only Cleage puts all theological doctrines totally within the context of the social. Sin is not a personal or individual attitude, but it is a social phenomenon. The same is true of redemption. Love is collective but limited to the soul brothers and sisters.

Community, or to be more exact, communalism, is stressed. It is a spirit of mutual support of and sharing with each other. Here one sees an attempt to recover one of the major aspects of the slave's "invisible institution" and of the free independent black church of the antebellum period. When a group of black members in the Johns Street Methodist Church, New York City, took the step that led to separation in 1796 and the establishment of the A.M.E. Zion Church, they gave as their reason for doing so: ". . . A desire for the privilege of holding meetings of their own, where they might have the opportunity to exercise their spiritual gifts among themselves, and thereby be more useful to one another." [37]

Most of these early black movements include the word "African" in their name, an indication of the stress on the communal spirit. With the ever-increasing black consciousness today, it is only natural for a theology evolving from the black experience to give a prominent place to the communal spirit. What we really have running through the thinking of the new breed black theologians is a concern for black identity. With Cleage it is communal identity only. With the others, particularly Vincent Harding, it is both personal and communal identity.

This paper by no means exhausts all of the implications of contemporary black theology. It does pinpoint the major emphasis: the theological doctrines of God, man, Jesus Christ, Holy Spirit, sin, redemption—all, are being set within the framework of the black experience.

Two other books dealing with the subject of this paper came to my desk too late to be thoroughly digested. Major J. Jones, president-director of Gammon Theological Seminary, Atlanta, has just published a book called *Black Awareness*. My brief scanning of it leads me to conclude that he has been greatly influenced by Jurgen Moltmann's work, *Theology of Hope*. But Jones follows the pattern of the others in correlating this hope with the black experience and postulates a theology of hope that will lead to a community beyond racism, but this is to be accomplished through the "unity in diversity" theme which appeared in Washington's third book.[38]

The second book which I have lately received is by J. DeOtis Roberts, professor of Christian theology, Howard University, Washington, D.C., and is entitled, *Liberation and Reconciliation: A Black Theology*. In his book Roberts stresses some of the same themes enunciated by the others. He sees again Black Power as an interim movement. But Roberts seemingly puts more emphasis on the doctrine of reconciliation than did the others. However, at the present time, he gives priority to liberation and says: "Liberation is the theme of Black theology. Christ is the liberator and the Christian faith promises 'deliverance of the captives.' It promises to let the oppressed go free." [39]

Although this theological strand of liberation that stands out in the "new breed" black theologian can be traced back to the "invisible institution" of the slaves and to the free black independent church of antebellum days, it has been left to the young black theologian of contemporary times to systematize this strand into a literate theology. I am proud that he accepted the challenge and is making known in an articulate manner the significance of a theology of relevance, for as Roberts so clearly points out, "he is attempting to understand the Christian faith in the light of his people's experience." [40]

8·The Black Church Revolution

OTIS MOSS, JR.

The Bible teaches us much about the concept of revolution. In the Gospel of Matthew Jesus gives us this statement. "Think not that I am come to destroy the law, or the prophets: I am not come to destroy, but to fulfil" (Matt. 5:17). *Today's English Version* translates this verse: "Do not think that I have come to do away with the Law of Moses and the teaching of the prophets. I have not come to do away with them, but to give them real meaning."

This, really, is the meaning of revolution in a Christian context. Many of us use the word without having an adequate theological and/or Christian understanding of it. We, therefore, run the risk of adopting other definitions of revolution which may or may not be what Christians ought to be saying when they talk about revolution.

Revolution, in a Christian sense, is the end of something, the fulfilment of something, and the beginning of something. If you want to examine the validity of any revolution from a Christian perspective, you must raise these questions:

What does the revolution bring an end to?
What does the revolution fulfil?
What does the revolution begin?

If it is simply an effort to gain a new position in an old world then it is not a revolution. This seems to be what most of us are working for. We are not trying to affect basic change, we just want to get on the staff in "Pharaoh's house." We are trying to get out of the "brickyard" and into the "palace." If you don't believe this, then watch the actions or reactions of those who are called from the

101

"brickyard" for a temporary appointment in the "palace." They change their rhetoric overnight. The folks you thought were marching with you begin to tell you how "you don't understand it."

"Excuse me, Brother, but I thought you were in the picket line on yesterday."

"Oh, but now is the time to change our strategy."

The challenge here is to reexamine what we really mean. Do we want a new world, or do we just want a new position in the old world?

What does the revolution you are involved in bring an end to? What does it fulfil? What does it start?

Some years ago there appeared an interesting and dynamic little book under the caption, *The Creative Revolution of Jesus: Then and Now.* Among other things, Kirby Page says that anyone who wants to understand the ministry of Jesus must be a student of revolution, for it was said by one of the contemporaries of Jesus that he wrought the most stupendous of revolutions. So if you want a revolution, start with Jesus. That's why some folk don't want Jesus. Richard Niebuhr said, "We want a Christ without a cross, a church without discipline, a God without wrath, a kingdom without judgment." But you can't have this and have revolution at the same time.

The revolution of Jesus brought an end, in one sense, to Hebrew and Pharisaic legalism. It fulfilled the prophecy and it started a creative movement upon this earth that all men since that time must be judged by. Even when you reject Jesus you must be judged by the things that he represents.

Revolution and Growth

Revolution, then, means growth, and growth is revolution. Am I involved in the revolution? Am I growing? Jesus talks about a grain falling into the ground and dying, and in the process of dying the grain of corn protests and breaks forth out of the ground and cracks it up. A new shoot comes forth and it grows. In the growth process it has to battle against the rain, the storm, and the sun while needing all of these at the same time. You must learn how to survive in the face of the thing you cannot get along without. You can't get along without the sunshine, but the sun can kill you if you are not quick. Have you ever heard of a sunstroke? You can't get along without sunlight, but the sunlight can blind you if you are not equipped to face it.

Am I a revolutionary? Am I growing? Revolution does not start from the outside. It starts from the inside and it must be based on revelation. Some folk have announced a revolution but they haven't had any revelation. Therefore, they are not building, they are stumbling and falling.

We stand today between the blind and the asinine. The asinine look at destruction and call it fulfilment. The blind look at growth and call it destruction. They call it destruction, because growth is painful. Try a real radical idea on your staff of deacons or trustees and you will see how painful a good idea can be. But don't just start there. Try a new one on yourself. "You shall know the truth and the truth shall make you free," but generally the truth will make you mad before it makes you free.

Christian education must speak to the issue of revolution and must guide us into an understanding of the Christian concept of revolution.

Revolution and Redemption

Redemption is the most revolutionary thing on earth. Redemption means freedom. There is a new political word today that often means salvation. We call it "liberation." But if you have your biblical understanding right, when someone starts talking to you about "liberation," you understand from a biblical and a theological point of view that they are talking about salvation. Don't let them upset you. You have something to tell them. You have a story to tell. Liberation means deliverance. Salvation means deliverance. It is the concept of freedom. If you have a revolution, what is it ending? What is it fulfilling? What is it beginning? If you have been converted, something ended in you. If you have been born again, something was fulfilled in you. Something is being fulfilled in you. If you have been born again something new in you got started.

I agree with E. Stanley Jones when he says that when a man is converted his vocabulary ought to be converted. You ought to have a new vocabulary. This is another way of saying that if you have been born again you ought to have some new words.

When I was twelve years old, I was a water boy at a Georgia sawmill. Interestingly enough, all the language in the ghetto that we call radical language, they were using all around those woods at the sawmill. Nobody wrote it down then. Even though it was not written down, one of the qualifications, I think, for holding on and holding out at the sawmill was to know how to say it real good. Now they weren't really cursing, they cussed. It was interesting enough at age twelve to get by without that kind of qualification, but you had to learn pretty fast.

There was one thing that I learned in that experience. The boss man and owner of the sawmill would walk around with a gun on his hip. He was really running a slave camp, a concentration camp. Because he recognized that his system was unjust, he carried with him that kind of equipment because he didn't know when a rebellion might get started or the idea might be put forth. So he had to be equipped to defend his injustice.

There was one worker whom they called "Speedy." They called him Speedy because he couldn't walk fast. He had bad feet. Speedy knew how to curse. He would curse all week long. Every time a tree fell wrong he would curse the tree out. The thing that I noticed was that it didn't matter how much he cursed the tree, it had no impact on the boss man. It didn't change his attitudes or any of our circumstances. While bad language made Speedy a big man among the workers, he was a failure in affecting change.

You can't stand in the "stables of Pharaoh" and curse your way to the "Promised Land." Somebody needs to inform all of us that cursing is not militancy. You can stand on 125th Street in Harlem and cuss all day long, and you won't affect the Dow Jones industrial averages at all.

Some people have confused what they call militant language with militant action. Cussing is not really radical. The stock market won't change because you call a white man some vulgar name. Nine times out of ten his wife called him that before you did. So don't feel that you have contributed to the revolution simply by calling some man a "pig." There is nothing revolutionary about that, but if you get hung up on that, you will end up looking like and acting like a pig yourself. It was an atheist who said, "When you deal with a monster beware lest you become a monster."

You see, if you fight with a skunk, at close range, on the ground; at his level, you will end up smelling like one, and when you walk down the streets of life the very odor from your body will spread the news that a skunk is in town. People will get confused on what you smell like and on what you are.

When a child is bitten by a rattlesnake, you don't help the child by cursing the snake. You help the child by dealing with the wound and coming to grips with the nature of the rattlesnake. You don't deal with a rattlesnake by crawling. You deal with a rattlesnake by being a man. You don't deal with a rattlesnake by merely using the language of frustration. We have confused the language of frustration with the language of liberation. We think we are being radical and militant, but we are expressing our own frustration.

Quite often when we get so mean and so bad, we don't end up intimidating anybody but each other. Some folk look so mean and bad. They even come to meetings and hang around the walls and look. They won't smile or say anything, just look mean and bad. They are trying to intimidate, but they have not yet dealt positively with the issue.

Eighty percent of the guns that black folk buy are used to shoot other black folk. One of the techniques of the slave master has always been to put outmoded guns in the hands of the slaves, in order that the slaves might shoot each other and keep themselves busy shooting each other while the slave master remains in control. One of the key instruments of the slave trade was firearms.

There were three passages in the slave trade: the outward passage; the middle passage; and the homeward passage. The outward passage can be illustrated by a ship leaving England with rum, cheap cloth, beads, and firearms. They went to the coasts of West Africa and exchanged the firearms, the rum, and the cheap beads for black cargo, human beings.

The middle passage was when they stopped at the islands and coasts of North and South America and exchanged the human cargo for sugar, cotton, and tobacco, and then began the homeward passage. We are the children of the middle passage. The slave master gave the coastal kings and some of the tribal chiefs guns and rum. Some of us now have .38's that haven't been greased good, and we are crying "revolution." We've got a .38 in one pocket and dope in the other pocket. Now that vetoes the possibility of even using that rusty .38. You don't have much target practice to start with; then when you got high on dope, you shot everybody but the enemy. But even if the gun had been in good shape, remember that the gun is still the instrument of the slave master. So violence is the most conservative form of initiating social change.

When some people say to me "nonviolence is impractical," I know then that we have fallen short in interpreting the meaning of nonviolence. When you speak about nonviolence to the average young person, they think you're talking about going out into the streets, leaning over and putting your head in front of a policeman's billy club, and letting him split your head wide open, and then you come back home bloody talking about you've been nonviolent. That is not necessarily nonviolence.

Nonviolence begins at home. How does a father relate to his children? How does a husband relate to his wife? How does a mother relate to her family. Nonviolence begins at home. That is the responsibility that is upon our shoulders as Christians.

We must give the right interpretations. Sometimes I hear people say, "But Brother Preacher that's dangerous." Of course it is dangerous. So is an automobile. How many people got killed in automobiles last year? Many more people got killed driving their automobiles with a license than people practicing nonviolence.

You will hear that "nonviolence is dangerous; it will get you hurt." So can a cigarette. Now, you meditate on that. Some folk claim that they are just so mad with white folk they want to kill them all. Yet they smoke the cigarettes that white folks make and own, and you don't even have to do that. You haven't even checked to see whether we have any good jobs in the tobacco industry. You just bought the cigarettes. You pass the word on that "Winston tastes good like a cigarette should." You can't stand the white man, so you say, yet you wrap up the brown tobacco in white paper and puff it out. Even the smoke is white.

Some of the meanest and worst folks I have ever met have not gotten mean enough to call a strike against Scotch whisky or bourbon, but they are just mad at the white man, and just ordered some more of his liquor. How many black folk are on the board of directors for the bourbon industry? You don't know, but you just hate whitey. At the same time you are slopping up his juice. Let's be consistent. Don't tell me that you despise the Englishman, but you love Scotch. He doesn't mind you despising him if that is the way you are going to act.

Revolution and Freedom

This leads me to the next point. Not only must we know the meaning of revolution, we must also know the meaning of freedom. Freedom means to be released from something, endowed with something, and related to something. If you release a man without any endowment, he is still a slave. If you don't believe that, you get released from your husband or wife or parents, with nowhere to go, nowhere to live, no money, no friends, no allies and see how free you are. If you are going to be released from bondage, you must be endowed with something to maintain your liberty. Otherwise, you might start looking back to Egypt. Like the children of Israel of old, you will complain about being brought out into a wilderness and wishing you were back in Egypt as slaves.

We must not only be endowed with something (this is the whole history of Reconstruction), but we must also be related to something. We must be related to God and to our fellowman; endowed with dignity and a reasonable portion of instruments that will enable us to have some degree of self-respect and self-determination.

Not only does revelation bring an end to something and the fulfilment of something and the beginning of something. Not only does the revolution concern itself with freedom, but the revolution is a conversion experience in a special way. It means that you ought to know the difference between symbols and substance. The cross is a symbol and I have some attachments to it. I don't mean in a sentimental way. If I confuse the symbol with the substance, I will end up worshiping the cross without knowing Jesus. The cross is a symbol. Jesus Christ is the substance. We must know the difference between symbol and substance. It is the business of Christian education to keep before us an eternal distinction between symbol and substance.

You see, this hair style which I have (an Afro) is a symbol, but what I have *in* my head is my substance. It is really foolish to walk around with an Afro hairdo and a "processed mind." Now I am with the Afro and I'll give you one reason why. It has moved us out of the "stocking cap" stage.

That was the stage in which we tried to make our hair conform to that which was not reality. To do this we wore a stocking cap all night long. We would have been much better off had we read a book for about ten minutes. But we wore the stocking caps on our heads all night long. That stocking cap kept our hair in a certain state of being for about fifteen minutes, and we went off often with a slick empty head. Now the one thing we must not do is make a transfer from a slick empty head to a bushy empty head. I'm with the symbol, and I can talk about it because I've got one.

We need the symbol of an Afro, but do we know anything about African culture? Do we know anything about what the Hebrews learned from the African? Do we know anything about the fact that some ideas found in Hebrew writings had already existed in Egyptian literature five or six thousand years before the Hebrew people got there? Do we know anything about the fact that an Ethiopian regiment came to the rescue of King Hezekiah, and historians say that it was at that point an African regiment saved the Jewish religion? Do we know anything about how Egypt and Ethiopia shook hands and gave the world a foundation for modern science? Gave the world the hour changing? Gave the world sandals? Gave the world organized religion through the development of the priesthood? I need not take more time at this point except to again raise the question, Beneath your symbol, what is your substance? Do you know anything about the empire of Ghana? Do you know anything about the empire of Mali? the University of Timbuktu? Beneath the symbol, what is your substance?

I have an African robe at home that I bought on the streets of Lagos, Nigeria. I have an African cane that I bought from a novelty shop in Accra, Ghana. These are symbols. When I put on my robe, the garment is my symbol, but my character is my substance. Beneath the symbol what about the substance?

Some of us have the symbols of revolution but not the substance of revolution. Some of us have the symbols of Christianity, but not the substance of the Savior. Revolution means that we know the difference between the symbol and the substance.

Revolution means, among other things, that we have a proper balance between love and criticism. One of the things that drives young people away from the church and from us is the fact that we have unloving critics on the one hand and uncritical lovers on the other. Sometimes church folk make the mistake of becoming unloving critics and sometimes parents make the mistake of being uncritical lovers. "Whatever *my* child does is all right." Now we mistakingly call that love. In order to fill the emptiness at Christmas and Easter we pile upon them all kinds of material trinkets to make up for the emptiness that came when we shirked the opportunity of discipline. What we need is critical love and loving critics. If you love me critically, you can also love me tenderly. If you love me tenderly, you make me to know what I can do. If you love me critically, you let me know what I can become.

The late Dr. H. H. Coleman of Detroit says that we have trained our children in how *to get*, but we have not trained up a child in how *to go.* "Train up a child in the way he should *go.*" But we have trained them in the way they should get. They know how to get everything, but they don't know how to go. They don't know how to go because *we* don't know how to go.

A revolution is a teaching experience. Some of us are walking around with a "hitmorized" agenda wrapped up in "niggerized" rhetoric designed by frustrated white folk. A lot of the methods that some black folk have that they think is black is really white. Some white folk, especially some young whites, turned the church off long ago, but the church never did represent to them what the black church represented to black folk. Some white folks got in the movement, and they were from First Baptist downtown. They began to define Shady Grove with the same bad definition that they had developed from First Baptist downtown. They got a lot of us confused. There are white folks who said to some of the black folks: "You ought to burn the church down because the church houses a Bull Conner, a Lester Maddox, and a George Wallace." But they weren't talking about *our* church. We didn't baptize the Bull Conners. We baptized the folk who challenged the Bull Conners.

The revolution is a teaching experience. The revolution ought to teach the meaning of concepts, phrases, and ideas. Some folk got scared to death (more black folk than white) over simple words like "Black Power," without knowing what it meant. When you get a classical definition of Black Power, you will find that it is an instrument for teaching. My definition of Black Power is black maturity; black maturity is economic security; economic security is political ingenuity; political ingenuity is functional ethnic unity. These must be built on books, bucks, and ballots, plus an indestructible self-appreciation and a sense of spiritual integrity.

The revolution is a teaching experience. It teaches that liberation is salvation; that freedom is redemption; that "right on" is a new "amen."

The revolution teaches that the church ought to be the focal point of radical idealism and creative realism. The church was made for the unfit, unholy, unrighteous, unworthy, and unready. The church was established to "comfort the afflicted and afflict the comfortable."

There are two necessary realities that must be present for a true revolution; love and truth. Nothing is more radical than love. Nothing is more militant and redeeming than truth. The church is the house of God only insofar as it is the house of love and the house of truth. When these realities are present in the church, we can speak with unlimited resources to everybody we meet and say: "Come and go with me to my Father's house."

9•Black and White Together

EMMANUEL L. McCALL

> For Christ himself has brought us peace, by making the Jews and Gentiles one people. With his own body he broke down the wall that separated them and kept them enemies (Eph. 2:14, *Today's English Version*).

America has been called "the melting pot of the world." Many cultures, languages, races, have cross-pollinated their ethnic identities. Anyone of us has learned to appreciate Italian pizzas, Mexican tortillas, German breads, Southern hominy grits, black soul food, English muffins, French pastries, ad infinitum. What we appreciate in food we have also appreciated in art forms, clothes, furniture, and some living styles.

By acculturation we have extracted the best of these subcultures, marketed them for what they had to offer, or synthesized them with other values.

We now stand at a religious juxtaposition. The black church tradition has several options before it. We can: (1) still deny that there is any worth in our religious expression and adopt only white styles of worship (Tomism); (2) seek to internalize our heritage and refuse to share it (separatism); or (3) select the best of our religious heritage, improve upon it, share it with others to help meet their needs, and at the same time receive the best that others have to offer and synthesize it to meet our needs (synthesis).

The white church stands at that same juxtaposition. It can: (1) continue to insist that only its heritage has worth and attempt to make everyone adopt it (paternalism); (2) continue to combine culture and religion for "white only"; or (3) share it best with others, receive the best from others, and creatively restructure for the glory of God and the good of each man (synthesis).

My conviction is that the church has the most solid theological, philosophical, and social bases for establishing community. In the past two decades athletics, business, entertainment, and government have made far more efforts than the church in helping us to be one. What has kept the church from leading in this effort? I suggest the following.

Christianity and Culture

The great tragedy of Western civilization is that we have tried to make culture and Christianity synonymous. This is currently evidenced by the attempts of Asian and African Christians to strip Christianity of its westernism and adapt it to their own particular cultures. We have seen how distorted Christianity can become when wedded to culture in the fact that the sustained perpetuators of racial animosity have sometimes been "good, upstanding, Bible-quoting, Bible-believing, church folk."

The effect of culturized Christianity can be evidenced especially from A.D. 312. On October 28, 312, Constantine and Maxentius were engaged in military conflict over the sovereignty of the Roman Empire.

On the night before, Constantine had a vision in which he saw the alphabetized symbol for Christ, the Greek letter "chi" superimposed by the letter "rho." The interpretation according to Constantine meant, "In this sign conquer." Constantine made a commitment that if this vision was an omen of victory and if victorious, he and his subjects would become Christians. This sounds like the cheap bargaining type of religious experience which Jacob had when he saw the vision of the ladder while he was fleeing Esau.

In the Battle of Mulvian Bridge, Constantine with the help of Licinius was successful. He *made* his soldiers become "Christian" because of the vision and the victory. In A.D. 481 Clovis, the Frankish monarch, had an experience leading to similar results.

To be sure, none of this could be considered authentic New Testament Christianity. No one can be made to become a Christian.

He may receive baptism and the privileges of church membership, but there will be no commitment to authentic New Testament faith or the Lord of the church. Such "Christians" will always prostitute the church to serve their own selfish ends. Thus "Christianity" as expressed by them will be accommodated to personal ambitions or desires. Church history is filled with illustrations of culturism in the name of Christ but lacking New Testament authenticity.

Since the Edict of Milan (A.D. 313) the church and culture have been in blending processes. There has often been fierce struggles to determine which would have the most influence. Because the church has not always consisted of or been lead by persons committed to the lordship of Jesus Christ, cultural whims, fancies, and expediences have dominated its life. Previous illustrations have already been given to show how the church in the South conspired with the culture to sustain slavery and its attendant evils.

Today we still hear such anachronisms as "God and country," "My country right or wrong." As late as September 6, 1971, the United Klans of America assembled in a pasture near Stone Mountain, Georgia, under the symbol of a "cross" with the theme song "The Old Rugged Cross."

Until we can learn to separate Americanisms and cultural adaptations from New Testament Christianity, the church of Jesus Christ will always be enslaved. Until we learn to examine our theologies and philosophies in light of the person and spirit of Jesus Christ, we will continue to grope in darkness. Until we accept the record of the life of Jesus Christ as the model for our daily living, the Holy Bible will be no more than an idol.

Approaches to Reconciliation

What can black and white Christians in America do to effect reconciliation?

1. I have already suggested that New Testament Christianity *be freed from the dominance of culture.*

2. We can *do away with paternalism.* We are not our brother's keepers. We are our brother's brother. A closer reading of the Cain

and Abel story in Genesis 4 will indicate that we have taken Cain's smart-aleck reply and tried to make it gospel. God has never said that we are to "keep" each other. To do so implies dominance and subservience of one or the other. If we "brother" each other, we recognize the freedom of each under God and his potential in being a son of God. Even Jesus Christ came as our "brother" not our "keeper."

Paternalistic feelings have expressed themselves since the days of slavery. Between white and black Baptists it has been expressed by: (1) giving property to blacks to build a church house; (2) giving money for the building, or building it; (3) occasional or regular contributions to the maintenance of the church and its facilities; (4) paying the salary of a black pastor; (5) establishing mission centers where valuables and foods are distributed to blacks; (6) contributing to the education of black ministers; and (7) giving support to black Baptist schools.

These have always meant a giving-receiving relationship, never the creation of purposeful fellowship among equals. Even the worship services of the past when interracially held, were carefully planned so that blacks did no more than sing. Rarely was a black invited to address the group. To do so would have meant that he expressed ideas. Ideas are dangerous if not controlled. Control is more easily maintained in a paternalistic setting. It was implied that if a man shares his ideas he could think and thus was an equal. In the society of the immediate past the goal was to be sure blacks did not become equal. Paternalistically controlled black churches have even dismissed pastors at the request of a white benefactor.

I have suggested that paternalism is a two-way problem. The other side of it is that there are some blacks who both desire and expect handouts from whites. They seldom speak their true feelings for fear of cutting off the benevolent supply. They will remain docile even in situations where constructive dialogue could be meaningful.

Now, younger and better-trained blacks are emerging as pastors of more and larger churches. The younger black is not looking for handouts. He will not be intimidated, nor will he remain silent in order to keep a supply line open. He will not accept only a singing role in any interracial service. The younger black has a theme which can be expressed thusly: "Give me a chance to earn an education and then to be gainfully employed on an equal par with anyone else, and I'll make it myself." This is not an appeal to separatism, but to the dignity and freedom of manhood.

This kind of black is in the ascendancy in America, but because he is not largely represented in the power structure of black denominational activities, his voice is seldom heard through those channels. Some older blacks, who are in the power structures, have allowed their white counterparts to assume that "our interracial work is doing just fine. Just keep the money flowing."

3. This leads me to *the problem of communication.* Our problem has several facets to it: (1) We have had faulty communication in the past because some whites wanted to be the only ones doing the talking. (2) We have had faulty communication because some blacks said only what they thought whites wanted to hear. (3) The problem today is in attempting to communicate with confused terminology.

Illustration: Many whites cringe with anger at hearing the term "Black Power." Immediately they assume this means "killing, looting, rioting," or they conjure up negative impressions of black extremist types. This is not the image of Black Power which most blacks have. As we use it, "Black Power is the cohesion of black people in order to strengthen our social, economic, and political destinies." This is nothing different from what generally goes on in any number of interest or lobby groups. In any given situation those possessing common interests bind together for effective, influential strength. There should be no valid reason for becoming uptight simply because blacks decide to make their own decisions about that which affects them. It is the lack of communication that causes us to be unnecessarily concerned and anxious about legitimate activities.

Illustration: Some white churchmen have become discouraged because they extended invitations to the black brethren to "come and have fellowship with us," but no one came. The use of the word "fellowship" is the first problem. Most whites use "fellowship" to mean a congenial gathering, complete with polite conversation, punch, and cookies. Blacks use the word "fellowship" with two emphases. First, they use it to mean the exchange of congregational involvement. Pastors and churches exchange services on special occasions usually with the visiting pastor delivering the message. Other involvements include cooperative activities between youth groups, WMU's and Brotherhoods, or other church relationships. Second, black churchmen use the word "fellowship" in reference to comradeship. It involves working, sharing, even suffering *together*. Generally, whites mean neither of these emphases in the common usage with interracial activities. The result of this communication gap is a confusion about purposes, reasons, and goals.

We must learn the basic principles of communicating for our day. These include purposeful listening, honest evaluation, creative input, definition of terms, the appropriate illustration of the terms defined, the willingness to talk *with* one another rather than *to* or *at*. Much of our verbage has been *at* or *to* each other instead of *with* each other.

The difference is not merely one of semantics. This was forcefully illustrated to me by a deacon at my Louisville pastorate. When he and another brother had had some hard words between them, he suggested that he was going to pray *with* the brother. Knowing the temperament of the second person involved, I asked whether the deacon thought he could succeed in getting the brother on his knees to join him in prayer, and if he succeeded would it be wise to close his eyes. The deacon responded by saying, "To pray *with* him means that I am going to try to see things from his point of view."

Racially we have been speaking *about, at,* and *to* each other too long. We must begin to talk *with* each other. This cannot be done in the absence of the other person. This cannot be done by merely reading or hearing about another person or situation. There must be personal, physical contact.

With this personal, physical contact may come anger, frustration, fear, or hostility. The initial meetings may be painful. Misunderstandings may or may not occur. But if one is persistent, he will discover the development of an openness, a freedom, an enlightenment that will add unknown dimensions of depth and learning. He will discover how valuable firsthand information is. He will discover how complicated we have made life through the use of traditional, mythologized fancies. He will discover new criteria for relationships with people. More importantly, he will find himself. Blacks will learn to "dig the white scene," while whites will learn to "dig the black scene." I have deliberately used the language of the youth culture for it describes what needs to happen. The word "dig" by common usage means to understand and to understand deeply. This is more than simply tolerating or coexisting. It includes personal involvement and commitment. One's whole being is brought into the new experience.

As we "dig the scenes," both black and white, we must seek to understand what each other thinks, says, and does. Once we understand, we must then commit ourselves to the courses of action most appropriate to our understanding, our resources, and our abilities. These courses must be "right on." The youth generation uses this term to mean "on target." It means that we have "zeroed in" on our priorities and are clear on our goals.

Once we have "dug the scene" and are "right on," we can expect the unexpected problems that can come from new ventures in race relations. We can expect isolation from those who disapprove, and disappointment with those who "cop out" (a quitter from a good and worthwhile cause); but if the task of racial reconciliation is to be forceful, men of faith must not abandon the struggle.

4. *"Let's get it all together."* The theme of this book is that the black religious tradition has something of value for America and the world. There now remains the task of "getting it all together." This is another phrase from the youth culture. I understand this term to mean the proper ordering of our priorities, getting our values straight, selecting the best that is to be found, and creating the best that can be made. It may mean borrowing from several sources in order to synthesize something better. As this relates to the black

church tradition, only black men can "get it all together" for blacks.

We must decide what in our tradition is most valid and significant. We must decide how best to share it. This does not mean that we can do so in isolation or exclusivism. There are skills, disciplines, philosophies, theologies, methods, and media techniques which others have developed and which we can appropriate to our own peculiar witness. We need the expertise of others. The disciplines of study, the products of past theological and philosophical research, the experience of business management, the priority of financial resources—all of this and more can be learned from the white church traditions. Black churchmen will profit by culling the best from the resources available and "getting it all together."

In the culling process we will especially need to decide what in the black church tradition is superfluous and what is of intrinsic value. Sometimes the expediency of the hour makes this decision for us. For example, the goal of most black preachers today is not just to leave a congregation shouting. Formerly this was an understood goal.

Today's preacher, often by pressure, has become more interested in the relationship of the gospel to crises and needs in the black community. Such a message calls for stimulation to action, not to shouting. This does not mean that emotional content is displaced. Emotional expression is still there, but shouting as such becomes a spontaneous occurrence rather than a sought-after goal.

It is not possible or desirable for any one or group to try to determine what is generally of intrinsic worth or what is superfluous for all others. Local areas have various uniquenesses which other locales do not have or do not share to the fuller degree. In any given area that which is of significance must be determined by those of that area. By accentuating the positive, we can eliminate the negative.

5. *"Spread the Sunshine."* This is the title of another song often used by the "now" generation. It is a plea for brotherhood, for sharing, for love, for meaning, and for purpose. The "sunshine" has always been symbolic of life, warmth, openness, health, joy, and

blessings. It is most valued after periods of winter or after cloudy skies.

Psychologically, America has experienced a decade of cloudy skies and even winter. We have become extremely polarized racially and seem unable to solve our problem. Somehow we lack the will. We have become isolationists with age differentials (generation gap). We have seen extended violence in numerous assassinations, mob killings, the destruction and maiming of lives both at home and in Vietnam. We have been shaken to despair at the extent and depth of our social problems, ghettos of poverty, illiteracy, unemployment, subcultures. We need "the sunshine." We need occasions to smile, to hope, to know more lasting joy, even while we still struggle with the despair of bad situations. Attempts are being made to bring in "the sunshine." Some are experimenting with new forms of worship. Some are developing extensive social programs. Some are turning to occult religions and even drugs as the panacea for this spiritual quest. Some are giving up altogether.

Out of the black church tradition can come the kind of life and vitality that will bless the whole of our land. Blacks have known well how to apply the gospel to the problems and needs of men, to be prophetic like Amos, Hosea, John the Baptist, and Jesus. Black churches have consistently moved to relate their resources to the solution of problems. Blacks have known how to sing, to be happy, to have inner peace, to have unusual joy even in the deepest despair. We, like the Israelites in Babylon, will fail God if we hang up our harps. Now is the time for someone to break forth with the music of Zion; not to entertain; not to commercialize; not to internalize; but to join God in his plan of world redemption.

Notes

Chapter One
[1] Howard Thurman, *The Luminous Darkness* (New York: Harper and Row, 1965).

Chapter Two
[1] Winthrop D. Jordan, *White Over Black* (Baltimore: Penguin Books, Inc., 1968), p. 179.
[2] *Ibid.*, p. 180.
[3] *Ibid.*, p. 181.
[4] *Ibid.*, p. 183.
[5] *Ibid.*, p. 188.
[6] *Ibid.*, p. 190.
[7] Harry V. Richardson, *Dark Glory* (New York: Friendship Press, 1947), p. 1.
[8] Jordan, *op. cit.*, p. 208.
[9] *Ibid.*, p. 210.
[10] *Ibid.*, p. 191.
[11] *Ibid.*, p. 191.
[12] Joseph R. Washington, Jr., *Black Religion* (Boston: Beacon Press, 1964), p. 182.
[13] Emmanuel L. McCall, *Centennial Volume* (Louisville, Kentucky: Standard Printing Co., 1968), p. 148.
[14] John Eighmy, "The Baptists and Slavery: An Examination of the Origins and Benefits of Segregation" *Social Science Quarterly*, December, 1968, pp. 666–673.
[15] *Ibid.*, pp. 666–667.
[16] Leonard H. Haynes, Jr., *The Negro Community Within American Protestantism*, p. 65.
[17] *Ibid.*, p. 114.
[18] Richardson, *op cit.*, pp. 14–15.
[19] Owen Pelt and Ralph Smith, *The Story of National Baptists* (New York: Vantage Press, 1960).

Chapter Six
[1] Carter G. Woodson, *The History of the Negro Church* (New York: Associated Publishers, 1921), p. 42.
[2] Joseph R. Washington, Jr., *Black Religion* (Boston: Beacon Press, 1964), p. 203.
[3] E. Franklin Frazier, *The Negro Church in America* (New York: Shocken Books, 1970), pp. 2–5.
[4] Frederic Bancroft, *Slave Trading in the Old South* (Baltimore: J. H. Furst Company, 1931).
[5] Carter G. Woodson, *The Negro in Our History* (9th ed. Washington, D.C.: Associated Publishers, Inc., 1947), p. 594.

Chapter Seven

[1] Henrietta Buckmaster, *Flight to Freedom*, p. 21.

[2] Preston N. Williams, "Black Church," *Andover-Newton Quarterly*, November, 1968.

[3] Robert N. Bellah, "Civil Religion in America," *Daedalus*, Winter, 1967.

[4] H. Richard Niebuhr, *The Social Sources of Denominationalism* (New York: Meridian Books, 1967), p. 3.

[5] Joseph R. Washington, Jr., *Black Religion* (Boston: Beacon Press, 1964), p. 289.

[6] Joseph R. Washington, Jr., *The Politics of God* (Boston: Beacon Press, 1969), p. xiii.

[7] *Ibid.*, p. xiii.

[8] *Ibid.*, p. xiii.

[9] *Ibid.*, pp. xiii–xiv.

[10] *Ibid.*, pp. 158–159.

[11] Joseph R. Washington, Jr., *Black and White Power Subreption* (Boston: Beacon Press, 1969), p. 124.

[12] *Ibid.*, pp. 126–127.

[13] *Ibid.*, p. 128.

[14] James H. Cone, *Black Theology and Black Power* (New York: Seabury Press, 1969), p. 117.

[15] James H. Cone, *A Black Theology of Liberation.* (New York: J. B. Lippincott, Co., 1970), p. 11.

[16] *Ibid.*, p. 17.

[17] Cone, *Black Theology and Black Power, op. cit.*, p. 121.

[18] *Ibid.*, p. 120.

[19] *Ibid.*, p. 126.

[20] Joseph A. Johnson, Jr., "Jesus the Liberator," *Andover-Newton Quarterly*, January, 1970, p. 89.

[21] *Ibid.*, p. 89.

[22] *Ibid.*, p. 89.

[23] *Ibid.*, p. 96.

[24] Vincent Harding, "The Religion of Black Power," Donald Cutler (ed.), *The Religious Situation* (Boston: Beacon Press, 1968), p. 7.

[25] *Ibid.*, p. 11.

[26] *Ibid.*, p. 11.

[27] *Ibid.*, p. 11.

[28] *Ibid.*, p. 13.

[29] Haywood Henry, Jr., "Toward a Religion of Revolution," *The Black Scholar*, December, 1970, p. 31.

[30] Harding, *op cit.*, p. 18.

[31] *Ibid.*, p. 25.

[32] Albert Cleage, Jr., *The Black Messiah* (New York: Sheed and Ward, Inc., 1968), p. 4.

[33] *Ibid.*, p. 4.

[34] *Ibid.*, p. 51.

[35] *Ibid.*, pp. 96–97.

[36] *Ibid.*, p. 7.

[37] Carter G. Woodson, *The History of the Negro Church* (New York: Associated Publishers, 1921), p. 67.

[38] Major J. Jones, *Black Awareness* (Nashville: Abingdon Press, 1971).

[39] J. DeOtis Roberts, *Liberation and Reconciliation: A Black Theology* (Philadelphia: Westminster Press, 1971), p. 32.

[40] *Ibid.*, p. 21.

Bibliography

Allport, Gordon. *The Nature of Prejudice.* Garden City: Doubleday & Company, Inc., 1954.

Ames, Russell. *The Story of American Folk Song.* New York: Grosset and Dunlap, Inc., 1960.

Cone, James H. *A Black Theology of Liberation.* New York: J. B. Lippincott Co., 1970.

Cone, James H. *The Spirituals and the Blues.* New York: Seabury Press, 1972.

DuBois, W. E. B. *The Souls of Black Folk.* Connecticut: Fawcett Publications, Inc., 1965.

Frazier, E. Franklin. *The Negro Church in America.* New York: Scarrett Books, Inc., 1962.

Grier, William H. and Cobb, Price M. *The Jesus Bag.* New York: McGraw-Hill Book Company, 1971.

Havlik, John F. *People-Centered Evangelism.* Nashville: Broadman Press, 1971.

Johnson, Joseph. *Soul of the Black Preacher.* Philadelphia: Pilgrim Press, 1971.

Jones, Major J. *Black Awareness: A Theology of Hope.* Nashville: Abingdon Press, 1971.

Jordan, Winthrop. *White Over Black.* Baltimore: Pelican Books, Inc., 1969.

Kelsey, George. *Racism and the Christian Understanding of Man.* New York: Charles Scribner's Sons, 1965.

King, Jr., Martin Luther. *Strength to Love.* New York: Harper and Row, 1963.

———. *Where Do We Go from Here: Chaos or Community?* New York: Harper and Row, 1967.

Knight, Walker. *Struggle for Integrity.* Waco: Word Books, 1969.

Lincoln, C. Eric. *Sounds of the Struggle.* New York: Friendship Press, 1967.

Mitchell, Henry. *Black Preaching.* New York: J. B. Lippincott Co., 1970.

Odum, Howard W. and Johnson, Guy B. *The Negro and His Songs.* New York: Negro Universities Press, 1968.

Owens, J. Garfield. *All God's Chillun.* Nashville: Abingdon Press, 1971.

Roberts, J. DeOtis. *Liberation and Reconciliation: A Black Theology.* Philadelphia: Westminster Press, 1971.

Thurman, Howard. *Jesus and the Disinherited.* Nashville: Abingdon Press, 1949.

Thurman, Howard. *The Luminous Darkness.* New York: Harper and Row, 1965.

Woodson, Carter G. *The History of the Negro Church.* New York: Associated Publishers, 1921.

Contributors

Otis Moss, Jr. is a native of Georgia, and he is pastor of the Mount Zion Baptist Church in Cincinnati, Ohio. He holds degrees from Morehouse College and Morehouse School of Religion. His previous pastorates were in LaGrange and Atlanta, Georgia, including Providence and Ebenezer Baptist churches in Atlanta. He also serves on the faculty of the University of Cincinnati. He is a frequent revivalist and lecturer on college campuses.

Leon L. Troy is a native of Ohio, and he holds degrees from the University of Toledo and Oberlin Graduate School of Theology. He has pastored churches in Ohio, including his present pastorate, Second Baptist Church, Warren, Ohio. He is involved in many educational pursuits. He serves on the Board of Trustees at Kent State University and the Warren Y.M.C.A. Board of Directors. He is president of the Ohio Baptist General Association, a state convention of black Baptists in Ohio.

Dearing E. King is a native of Tennessee. He holds degrees from LeMoyne College in Memphis, Howard University Graduate School, Howard University School of Religion, and Simmons University. He has pastored churches in Paducah and Louisville, Kentucky, and New York City. Presently he is pastor of the Monumental Baptist Church in Chicago, and president of the Progressive Baptist State Convention of Illinois.

Henry H. Mitchell is a native of Ohio. He holds degrees from Lincoln University in Pennsylvania, Union Theological Seminary in New York, Fresno State College in California, and Covina Campus, American Baptist Seminary of the West. He has served the black church from Harlem and Brooklyn to Los Angeles and San Francisco. His specialties at various times have included bilingual work (Spanish), church extension, black employment campaigns, the war on poverty (chairman of CAP Agency), human relations consultant for school boards, and a variety of writing assignments in Christian education and human relations. He is the author of the recent book *Black Preaching*. He is presently professor of black church studies at Colgate-Rochester Divinity School and Crozer Theological Seminary in New York.

Joseph C. Pyles is a native of Alabama, and he is presently pastor of Pleasant View Baptist Church, Louisville, Kentucky. He has also had pastorates in Indiana. He serves as professor of church music at Simmons Bible College. He received his training from Montgomery State Teachers College, Indiana University, and Simmons University Bible College.

W. J. Hodge is a native of Texas. He is a graduate of Southern University, Baton Rouge, Louisiana, and Oberlin Graduate School of Theology in Ohio, with additional study at Garrett Biblical Institute, Evanston, Illinois, Louisville Presbyterian, and the Southern Baptist Theological Seminary in Louisville. He has had faculty positions at Lynchburg Theological Seminary in Virginia and Simmons University. Presently he is the Urban Program Director of the Louisville Chapter of the NAACP and pastor of the historic Fifth Street Baptist Church.

John W. Fleming is a native of North Carolina. He has training from Shaw University, with graduate degrees from Oberlin Graduate School of Theology in Ohio. He has directed Christian education for the state of North Carolina and has pastored several churches in North Carolina. For a number of years he has been on the faculty of Shaw University. At present he is an associate professor of African and Afro-American studies at Shaw and a lecturer at Southeastern Baptist Theological Seminary in Wake Forest.

Emmanuel L. McCall is a native of Pennsylvania. His educational preparation was at Simmons Bible College, University of Louisville, and Southern Baptist Theological Seminary in Kentucky. He served on the faculty of Simmons Bible College for ten years and as pastor of the Twenty-eight Street Baptist Church in Louisville for eight years. Presently he is associate secretary of the Department of Work with National Baptists, Home Mission Board, Southern Baptist Convention in Atlanta, Georgia. He serves as visiting professor of Christian ethics at Southern Baptist Theological Seminary in Louisville. He is the editor of four books and writer for numerous periodicals and publications.